Trade to Win

Founded in 1807, John Wiley & Sons is the oldest independent publishing company in the United States. With offices in North America, Europe, Australia, and Asia, Wiley is globally committed to developing and marketing print and electronic products and services for our customers' professional and personal knowledge and understanding.

The Wiley Trading series features books by traders who have survived the market's ever changing temperament and have prospered—some by reinventing systems, others by getting back to basics. Whether a novice trader, professional, or somewhere in, between these books will provide the advice and strategies needed to prosper today and well into the future.

For a list of available titles, visit our Web site at www.WileyFinance.com.

Trade to Win

Proven Strategies to Make Money

THOMAS L. BUSBY
with
PATSY BUSBY DOW

WILEY

John Wiley & Sons, Inc.

This book is dedicated to Melvin T. Busby, my dad, who is a great father, grandfather, and uncle. His advice has propelled me to work hard and strive to improve. His smile and soft-spoken manner has endeared him not only to his family, but many others with whom he has come in contact throughout the 80 plus years of his life.

Published by John Wiley & Sons, Inc., Hoboken, New Jersey.
Published simultaneously in Canada.

For general information on our other products and services or for technical support, please contact our Customer Care Department within the United States at (800) 762-2974, outside the United States at (317) 572-3993 or fax (317) 572-4002.

Wiley also publishes its books in a variety of electronic formats. Some content that appears in print may not be available in electronic books. For more information about Wiley products, visit our web site at www.wiley.com.

Library of Congress Cataloging-in-Publication Data:

Busby, Thomas L., 1951–
  Trade to win : proven strategies to make money / Thomas L. Busby with
Patsy Busby Dow.
      p.   cm.—(Wiley trading series)
    Includes index.
    ISBN 978-0-470-28534-3 (cloth)
  1. Speculation.   2. Investments.   3. Risk management.   4. Investment analysis.
I. Dow, Patsy Busby.   II. Title.
    HG4521.B84   2009
  332.64′5—dc22   2008023263

Printed in the United States of America.
10   9   8   7   6   5   4   3   2   1

Contents

Foreword

Trade to Win would seem to be the only reason to be in the markets. However, I have found from my more than 40 years of association with traders and investors, that it is not the case. In fact, I have found that traders and investors talk about winning and their individual wins, when they are, in fact, overall losers. I am reminded of a trader from the 1985 soybean market, who after making a potential huge profit gave it all back because she didn't want to sell "her" beans.

I met Tom Busby several years ago. I was immediately impressed with his low key, down-to-earth, and confident demeanor. His approach to the markets and to trading was matter-of-fact and simple to understand. He makes a trade for only one reason—to make money. And once his objective is met, he exits. He doesn't need to be in the markets just for the sake of being there.

Trade to Win is a roadmap to build a trader's winning attitude. It is easy to read and easy to follow. While reading the pages, your confidence will swell as you gain insight into how you may overcome your biggest trading obstacle, yourself. Tom reassures you that it is okay to win—and to win quickly. He helps you understand the risks involved in trading while also teaching you methods to forecast and mitigate market disasters.

It is so refreshing to read about a person who admits to making mistakes and withstanding a disaster that wiped him out. Tom does just that while detailing his struggle to regain his confidence in the markets and his ability to trade again and to win. After the markets dealt him a near deadly blow, he persisted and built a successful career as both a trader and an educator. All through the text, Tom offers "pearls" of knowledge that are the foundation for understanding trading and the markets. He adds still more by showing the reader specific trade ideas and the importance of timing in achieving success.

Over the years I have worked with many trading advisors and Tom Busby is the only one who has been willing to make a live trade in front of a live audience. He puts his money where his mouth is; he is one of a kind.

When he says he can show you how to make your trading day in twenty minutes, he means it, and I have seen him do it.

It is all about education. We are not born traders. Understanding the basics all the way to the psychology of trading is a learned ability. Tom is a master trainer. *Trade to Win* will help you build the discipline and skills that make the trading game understandable, and his strategies will prepare you to make money.

To win you need to stay in the game. Chapter 17 sets you up to stay for the long haul. Risk management is the most important lesson a trader can learn. Quickly identifying when trades are bad and cutting your losses fast, using stop/loss orders, and knowing before you place a trade the amount of money that can be lost—all of these strategies help manage risks. Not all of your trades will be winners. The key to successful risk management is knowing quickly which trades are losers and letting them go.

My favorite chapter is "Psychology and Discipline: The Winner's Edge." This is where the rubber meets the road. You can't win if you won't let yourself win. That's right, most traders don't believe they are good enough to win; the markets are too tough. Tom sets the tone for you to think like a winner, and be a winner from the start. The markets are here for us to make money, not just the professionals, but for us, all of us, and that means you!

Discipline is the backbone and muscle required to win. Tom Busby is the most relaxed, confident trader I have ever met. His confidence is a product of his discipline. He has developed this discipline over a lifetime of trading. Much of his discipline was gained as a by product of getting beaten up by the markets. If you read his teachings and put his lessons into practice, you may be able to avoid the hard blows that the markets can deliver. As a trader myself, I wrote my rules out and kept them next to my screen and reviewed them every day to keep me disciplined.

In a recent interview, I was asked if I would give just one piece of advice to a trader starting out. I replied, "I would tell him to read and heed Tom Busby's *Trade to Win*."

NED W. BENNETT
CEO, optionsXpress, Inc.
Executive Vice Chairman, optionsXpress Holdings, Inc.
September 2008

Preface

I have waged a lifelong battle with Wall Street. I placed my first trade almost three decades ago. Since that time I have made literally thousands of trades in a variety of markets. I have traded stocks, bonds, options, futures, commodities, and U.S. and foreign products. In my youth I never imagined that I would become a professional trader. However, once I began trading, I was hooked. In years past I was employed by some of the major brokerage houses. However, today I trade for myself and I teach trading to others. My school, DTI, is more than 10 years old. Students come to DTI from around the United States and some even come from foreign countries to learn the art of trading.

Over the years the DTI staff and I have taught hundreds of students. One of them, Charlie Prince, stands out in my mind because Charlie wanted to learn all that he could. It seems that it was not Charlie who initially had such a keen interest in his studies, but his wife. She was the driving force behind him and his trading education. His wife brought Charlie into my office and explained that it was important for him to understand how to invest and manage their money so that they would be able to enjoy their retirement. She planned to spend her days walking down some sandy beach and relaxing. Money was needed to achieve that goal and she made that crystal clear to both Charlie and me. Luckily, Charlie was willing and able to take on the task. He said that he would work as hard as necessary and take as many courses as needed to learn the information that would give him personal control over his financial destiny. Charlie enrolled in a class and has been returning to DTI and learning ever since. Charlie understood both then and now that empowerment comes through education.

Trading is not easy, and I have suffered my fair share of setbacks and losses. But, I have learned from my experiences and I am a survivor. I enjoy trading. Every morning when I slip out of bed, I know that new challenges will face me. I do not fear those challenges—I look forward to them. I do not make a fortune every day, but all of my trading days combined generate a good living for my family and me. Trading allows me to live my life on my terms.

This book is divided into three parts. Part One explains the fundamental elements of my trading approach. It deals with the significance and use of time, key numbers, and market indicators. It also explains how these elements of trading work together to properly read the tape and understand the language of the markets. Part Two details specific trading strategies. You will find strategies for trading stocks, options, futures, and other financial products. If you have ever traded, you know the importance of risk management, money management, and emotions in successful trading. Without them, the best strategy will fail. Furthermore, Part Three offers guidance and strategies for putting all of the elements of trading together to enable you to approach the financial markets with more wisdom and more strength. It is my hope that Chapter 18 will be especially helpful to you. It deals with real-world psychology to assist you in having the discipline to succeed.

Trading to win is a mind-set. Those who succeed in the financial marketplace are the ones that expect to do so. They do not win by accident. They learn about the markets. They work at their craft. As markets and technologies change, they change with them. There are two ways to gain lessons from Wall Street: let the market beat you up and teach you, or learn from someone who has taken the licks and teaches from experience. Through these pages readers have the opportunity to learn vicariously from a person who made his first losing trade in the late 1970s but was not turned off by Wall Street—a person who is a professional trader, daily doing battle with the bulls and the bears of the financial markets.

Throughout the text are 31 Pearls of Wisdom. They are numbered and scattered in text boxes as applicable throughout the book. Take note of these as they will aid you in your quest for success. I hope you find the information in these pages helpful and that it will assist you in improving your consistency and your profits.

THOMAS L. BUSBY

Acknowledgments

The students and staff of DTI are major contributors to this book. When I work with students, they have much knowledge and insight to share. As we strive together to understand the markets and trade effectively, we learn from each other and that knowledge is shared in these pages. In addition to my many students who challenge me and show me new approaches to old problems, the staff at DTI is also responsible for many of the ideas in these pages. Chuck Crow assisted with graphics. Geof Smith contributed ideas and assisted with edits. Jeanette Sims keeps the company going on a day-to-day basis and works hard to keep us all on track. Patsy penned the book and worked hard to explain my strategies and ideas. Petra Gross, a student and friend, assisted with editing and I thank her for her excellent editing. To all of them, I say "Thank you." I appreciate each of you.

I would also like to thank Paula, my wife of 25 years, my sons, Winston and his wife Casey, and Morgan and his wife Melanie. They are the ones who have always believed in me and have given me the fortitude to keep learning and trading. And, of course, there is Maggie, my bulldog and friend who is my trusted early-morning and late-night trading companion.

T. L. B.

PART ONE

A Foundation for Success

CHAPTER 1

The Trader's Edge

I was in Las Vegas. The year was 2003. I was conducting a seminar at a large financial event attended by traders and investors from around the country. The attendees came to the desert hoping to learn more about the markets. I was standing in the front of the room finishing the last details of preparation for my presentation when the crowd began to gather. I could not help myself; I began eavesdropping on some of the conversations. In my defense, it was almost impossible not to do so because the capacity-filled room of 1500 participants seemed to magnify the voices near me. Repeatedly, I heard the same refrain echoing around the dimly lit room: the bursting tech bubble in 2000 had been devastating. Noting the gray on their heads and lines of wisdom on their faces, I realized that many of these attendees were either retired or approaching retirement. They had apparently trusted professionals to handle their investments. As the new century began, their portfolios were heavy with techs and dot-coms. With the high-tech sector experiencing such meteoric gains, the folks in my audience had been relying on those investments to fund happy idle days filled with gardening, cruising, playing with the grandkids, and just enjoying life. Then the dot-com crisis destroyed their plans.

On March 10, 2000, the Nasdaq hit an intraday high of 5132.52. The bulls had been pushing prices up since 1999. Investors and traders loved the Internet technology that led to the formation of many dot-com companies. During the year before the crash, market value in the tech-heavy Nasdaq had doubled in value. These listed corporations offered a variety of products and services—some practical and some not. Many of them did not follow traditional business models. Even those that had never turned a

3

profit attracted investors and dollars flowed into their coffers at unprecedented rates. Just one year before the bubble burst, I boarded a bus in Beaver Creek, Colorado. I was taking a short hop from the slopes to my lodge. While I was on the bus, a popular dot-com company moved up 10 points—10 points in value in minutes. That particular Wall Street darling that enjoyed the spotlight in the late 1990s is now defunct. Few of today's traders would even recognize its name. Based on the conversations I was hearing in Vegas, some of the money lost in the dot-com fiasco had obviously come from people sitting in front of me.

On Friday, March 10, 2000, investors were happy. Their high-tech gamble seemed to be paying off for them. Then Monday, March 13, came. The U.S. markets gapped down at the open and headed south. Initially, the drop was not excessively dramatic—about 10 percent loss of value over the course of several days. Many analysts hoped that a correction might be good for the markets and prices would stabilize. But the bears were relentless and the fall did not end. Tech stocks continued to decline in value for many months. By October 2002, $5 trillion in market value in tech stocks was gone. Month after month high techs experienced a slow but steady downward bleed. As Figure 1.1 depicts, the Nasdaq took a beating in 2000 and has not recovered to precrash levels. In fact, at the time of this writing, it has not even recovered to the 50 percent level.

I remember going to Cozumel the year the bubble popped. I met a man from Florida who was a police officer. He was living it up, enjoying the sun, smoking expensive cigars, and bragging about his investment in an Internet

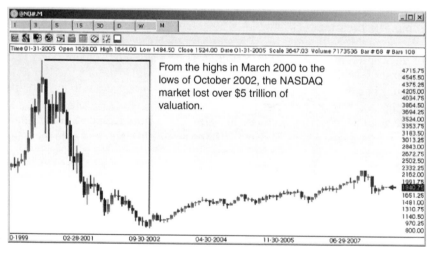

FIGURE 1.1 The Nasdaq's drop in 2000 and its slow struggle back. Eight years later it still has a long way to go to reach those early 2000 highs.

company. He claimed to have bought some stock for $10 a share, and he said it was currently trading for $200 a share. When I asked him some basic questions about his investment, like the products and services the company produced or provided and other such simple information, he looked at me like I was a fool and admitted that he really knew little about it. His investment was a great one, and he was holding on to it for the long term. It was his ticket to wealth. I remember thinking that the policeman was evidence that the bubble was about to burst. If a policeman who admitted that he knew nothing about the stock market was seeing his Internet investment go from $10 to $200, something was about to happen and it was not going to be good. When I think of that guy now, I wonder how his investment was faring in October 2002.

I suspect that the Florida cop crashed and burned like so many others. Clearly, a lot of the folks in the room in Vegas were also on the losing team in 2000. I heard them speak of portfolios cut in half and retirement funds wreaked. As the stories were repeated, many admitted that they had listened to fast-talking brokers and advisers who lured them into feelings of security and trust. They asked few questions and lived to regret it. This was not a happy group. They were skeptical, and with good reason. They and their portfolios had taken a beating.

As I started my presentation on that day in Vegas, it was important to offer them some good advice. I wanted to help my listeners make money and regain confidence in themselves and their abilities. I believed that I had some valuable information to share. I identified with the pain in their faces because I, too, had personally experienced the devastation of a huge financial loss. Not in 2000, but years before. As the room in Vegas came to life, I remembered those terrible days.

On October 19, 1987, I was living in Oklahoma City working as a vice president for a large brokerage house. At that time I had been a broker for a number of years specializing in trading futures and options. In fact, I was one of the largest retail options traders in the United States. With the right play, a lot of money can be made in options. But greed and mistakes can be costly. The month before the crash, I assisted my biggest client in making a million dollars. That is a million dollars of green in one month. On Black Monday, he lost that million and much more.

Making money seemed so easy before that fateful trading day over two decades ago. On August 25, 1987, the Dow Jones hit a high of 2722, and the markets seemed unstoppable. When I left the office on Friday afternoon, October 16, I thought I was king of the mountain. I, a small-town boy from Mobile, Alabama, was beating Wall Street. Little did I know that within a few days the Dow Jones would drop more than 500 points and lose more than 22 percent of its market value! In fact, such a thought was unimaginable to me. Friday's market had been very active, but I saw no

FIGURE 1.2 The dramatic Dow drop on Black Monday in 1987. On that date the Dow Jones fell more than 500 points representing a loss of more than 22 percent of its market value in a single day.

signs of collapse. When Monday's trading began, I initially saw no signs of panic. However, a real sell-off came in the afternoon and the madness began. From those highs in August (2722), prices quickly tumbled to a low of 1739. The huge drop in the United States reverberated around the globe. To the north, south, east, and west the pain and panic spread. A look at the Dow Jones chart visually depicts the 1987 crash. The numbers cannot begin to convey the pain suffered. Figure 1.2 captures the dramatic price drop that translated into financial disaster for me and for millions of others.

Many folks view Black Monday in 1929 as our market's most severe crash. In fact, in 1987 the financial markets experienced their greatest single-day percentage price drop in our nation's history. It is true that the long-term effects of the 1929 crash were more severe and extensive. Following the 1920s plunge, our nation fell into a deep depression that lasted for years. In contrast, in 1987, the Dow started on the road to recovery relatively quickly. Nevertheless, the yearly highs of August 1987 were not seen until 1989. Even though the downward dive was brief, the impact of 1987 landed a devastating blow to many traders and investors, and I was one of those left bloody. I know now that the key to avoiding such a disaster in the future is education and more education. Keep studying and improving. And, above all else, respect risk.

On that historic date in 1987, I was short approximately 1000 S&P 100 puts. That is, I had sold about 1000 options that I did not own. I had guaranteed the buyers of the puts that I would produce the underlying stocks if the strike price of the options was hit. In the melee, the strike price was hit and I was obligated to produce. That meant that I had to buy the shares at a preset high price and deliver them to their rightful owners. Never mind that the market had fallen like a meteor dropping across a vast Montana sky. Never mind any excuse or rationalization—I had to deliver on my deal. Survival, the basic instinct of mankind, became the dominant motivation of the day. Brokerage houses, fearful that they may not survive, forced customers to immediately liquidate positions and, in many cases, meet huge margin calls. Watching the clients ante up was like seeing lambs led to the slaughter.

On Black Monday there were so many orders hitting the exchanges that the computer systems were unable to execute them. According to John Phelan, the chairman of the New York Stock Exchange at the time, about 600 million shares traded that day. Unfortunately, that was about 200 million shares more than the processing capacity of the industry. (See *Fortune*, online edition at CNNMoney.com, "Remembering Black Monday," Corey Hajim and Jia Lynn Yang). The exchanges were forced to close in order to sort things out. For some time, traders were in the dark about their trades and their accounts. Had the orders that they had placed during the panic been filled? If so, at what price? Was a margin call due? If so, how bad was it? Those were scary times.

Such uncertainty added to the tension and fear. Both my clients and I had to nervously wait and worry for days before we knew the total extent of our losses. Once I learned the truth, it was not a pretty sight. I, of course, was not alone. Many of my clients were also badly hit, and that was very painful for me. Personally, I was broke. I had to sell basically all of my assets and start again. My nice car, my beautiful home—all of my hard-earned and valuable possessions were gone.

Folks who know me are aware of my fondness for trading futures like the S&P, Dow, and Nasdaq. I'll tell you one reason that I value futures. In addition to options, I was also trading some futures contracts to help me hedge my position when Black Monday hit. Had it not been for those futures contracts, I would have been forced to file for bankruptcy. I lost a lot, but my futures play was my lifeline. I would have been completely finished had I not done some hedging maneuvers with futures.

My investment portfolio was in ruins, but the loss of worldly goods was not my only problem and certainly not my biggest. I lost my sense of trust in the financial markets. And I lost faith in myself and my ability to make a living in the arena that I loved. Incidentally, to gain a respect for the resiliency of our financial markets, consider that the Dow high in 1987 was around 2750. Currently, the Dow is trading in the 12,700 area—a big upward move since those sad days of 1987.

THE ROAD TO VEGAS

I did not know how much money the folks in my audience in Vegas had lost with the 2000 crash, but I knew many of them had lost a significant amount and they were seeking answers. After 1987, I, too, sought answers. Not long after the collapse, I left Oklahoma City and headed east to my hometown, Mobile, Alabama. For some time, I struggled both financially and emotionally. I tried to regain my footing and my confidence. I traded, but my fear prevented me from making the right moves. I wanted to make money but was paralyzed by fear. I was going through a difficult time, but I continued to study the markets and work hard analyzing them. Gradually, with a lot of effort, patience, and persistence, I began developing a different trading strategy that respected risk. I still hoped to make money, but with each trade I considered the risk associated with the trade first. If the risk was too great or if I could not afford the potential loss, I did not take the trade. It was a new approach for me. It was that background and knowledge that I stood ready to share with those investors and traders who were disillusioned in Las Vegas in 2003.

Much of my trading focuses on indexes like the S&P 500. Rarely, a day goes by that I do not trade the S&P 500 futures. Some readers may not be familiar with this product. It is an equity index futures contract, and its value is derived from the cash value of the S&P 500. I see this futures contract as a way to trade the value of the stocks listed on the S&P index without actually buying or selling corporate shares. These are futures contracts, and trading them involves unique risks but also offers unique rewards. I explain these advantages and disadvantages later in the book. Just suffice it to say here that I am known as an S&P trader, and many of my listeners in Vegas in 2003 expected me to make recommendations about S&P trading. They were surprised when I shifted gears and suggested they look at gold.

Because I am a trader, I track and trade a variety of financial products. If I see an opportunity in commodities, I trade that area of the market. If equities or options appear to be ripe for profits, I look there. During the course of my career, I have traded equities, options, futures, precious metals, fuels, agricultural products, and anything else I could find that offered money-making potential.

At the time I was speaking in Vegas, one of my dearest friends and most loyal clients was Dr. Smith. Dr. Smith had a fascination for gold and for years had wanted to find a buying opportunity. With a great deal of persistence, I had steered him clear of the precious metals market because I did not believe money could be made there. Year after year the bulls faced losses, and year after year I kept the good doctor away from that particular arena. However, I always followed prices in precious metals both because I was looking for the right time to buy and because gold can be used as a market indicator. (I will tell you more about the significance of gold as an indicator in Chapter 4.)

On this particular date, I saw signs that an upward move in gold and precious metals was likely. Therefore, I did not suggest that the audience trade the indexes, but rather I recommended a metals play. Specifically, I told the group that if they took a long position in gold or silver they should be able to make some money and pay for their Vegas trip. The specific stocks I suggested were ASA Limited and Hecla Mining. Both Hecla (HL) and ASA (ASA) are traded on the New York Stock Exchange. Hecla is one of the oldest silver and gold mining companies in the United States. ASA Limited was founded in the 1950s. These corporations were not flash-in-the-pan businesses.

Much to my delight, before leaving Vegas, several of the show's participants approached me to report that they had taken my advice and gone long gold. The play had paid and they were ready to listen to more of my market musings. Not only had these skeptics made a little money, but they had also regained some of their lost faith. In fact, some of the people who sat in that audience in Vegas are still trading today and are students at DTI, the trading school I founded in Mobile. They have learned that with the right market plays, money can be made on Wall Street. Ron McDow, a student and one of those who watched that gold trade in Vegas, later noted that the market truly pays for knowledge.

Gold has been experiencing a bullish run since 2003. Figure 1.3 is a chart of mini gold futures. It shows the steady sharp climb of gold from 2003 to the present. There have been some small and brief corrections and consolidation periods, but the overall trend has been up. I have traded gold many times since that Vegas conference.

BECOMING A TRADER

My experience with trading equities goes back a little further than that 2003 trip to Vegas. I made my first equity trade in the late 1970s. I was serving my country in the U.S. Air Force and was stationed in Madrid, Spain. I

FIGURE 1.3 I, like others, have been bullish on gold for years. And, as the mini gold futures chart shows, the market has proven us right.

knew almost nothing about the stock market, but had a pal who traded pork bellies. Every day he bragged about all the money he was making. I had no clue as to how to trade pork bellies or anything else, but not wanting to be outdone, I decided to open a stock account and make a purchase. I thought that Merrill Lynch was the only brokerage house in the world. At least it was the only one that I had ever heard about. So, I made my way to downtown Madrid, the capital and most populated city in Spain. I located the Merrill Lynch office and opened an equity account. I knew so little about the markets that I thought I could trade pork bellies with a stock account. Little did I know that I had to open a commodities account for that particular trade. At any rate, I had an account and I was in the game.

Because I was associated with the aeronautical branch of the military, I purchased shares in two air carriers: Eastern Airlines and Pan Am. My purchases seemed logical to me at the time, and I made no analysis of either company or their financial performance. In those days, I had never heard of real-time market quotes and had no means of obtaining timely price data. Few individuals did, and certainly not a serviceman stationed in Spain. My financial numbers came from a military publication, *The Stars and Stripes*. The prices quoted in the publication were days old. Nevertheless, I always checked the stock section and noticed how my holdings were trading.

Regardless of whether they were up or down, I was proud to be a share-holder. Like my pal, I also bragged about my market acumen.

Truth is, my first venture into the markets did not serve me well. Both Pan Am and Eastern Airlines no longer exist, but I still have some of my shares. They are hanging in the classroom of my trading school in Mobile, Alabama. They decorate a small section of a rear wall and are concrete evidence of my long and hard battle with the bulls and bears of Wall Street. How many times have you made a "logical" decision that turned out to be not so logical at all? At least those shares ended up being of some value. They add a personal touch to the classroom décor and evidence my first attempt to be a market player. Admiral Nimitz, the commander-in-chief of Pacific Naval Forces during World War II, once said, "Every dog deserves two bites." I'm glad I got my two bites at the markets because my second one paid off for me. Figure 1.4 is a photograph of my Pan American Airways stock.

Shortly after my stock purchase in Madrid, I completed my stint with the military and moved to Oklahoma City. I had a day job and attended law school in the evenings. Because I had enjoyed trading equities, I

FIGURE 1.4 This was one of my first stock purchases. I bought 35 shares of Pan American Airways.

contacted the local Merrill Lynch office and began spreading my wings again. This time, my broker, Henry, suggested that I trade options. Oil prices were soaring, and Henry traded oil options on a regular basis. He taught me his strategy and I, too, became a player. Henry espoused the Bigger Fool Theory. That is, he believed that he could buy oil options at almost any price and still find a "Bigger Fool" to pay a higher price for them. The strategy was simple. If an oil stock rose in price on one day, we bought the options on the second day, and sold them on the third day. Henry was a great mentor, and his plan worked time after time. I just kept following Henry's lead and making more money. I now know why the system worked so well. When prices are at their highs, they tend to make higher highs. And, when they are at their lows, they tend to make lower lows. When a financial product is on fire, buying the highs is not such a bad idea. I made money over and over again by following Henry's strategy.

PEARL 1

When prices are trading at their highs, they tend to make higher highs, and when they are trading at their lows, they tend to make lower lows.

I had such success with my system that one day I received an invitation to lunch from the office manager. He had learned of my victories and asked me to join the firm as a broker. It was an idea that I had not previously entertained. I anticipated completing my law degree and entering the legal profession. But the firm offered me the chance to complete my degree at night and work for the brokerage house during the day. After much soul searching and arm twisting, I accepted the offer. However, I still planned to complete law school and eventually practice law. In the meantime, I would trade the markets. In fact, I finished law school, but never left the financial field. I eventually moved from Merrill Lynch but continued working for other firms. Trading the markets was my profession and I enjoyed it. That is, I enjoyed it until the crash of 1987. Then my life flipped upside down.

Most people in this business enjoy talking about the millions they make. I focus on the losses I have suffered and the lessons that I have learned. By using past experiences to gain insight and knowledge in the present, I am able to enjoy the rewards of trading for the long term. At the time of this writing, DTI has just ended an anniversary class. My students and I spent a week demonstrating how to turn losers into winners.

PEARL 2

Think of trading as a journey. Enjoy the trip and continuously learn from it.

THE AFTERMATH OF BLACK MONDAY

Not long after the crash, I left Oklahoma City and headed east to my hometown, Mobile, Alabama. Like a bird returning to its nest, if I had to start over, home was where I had to go. For some time, I struggled both financially and emotionally. I tried to regain my footing and my confidence. I traded, but my fear prevented me from making the right moves. I wanted to make money but was paralyzed by fear. I was going through a difficult time, but I continued to study the markets and work hard analyzing them.

Each morning when I slipped out of bed I felt defeated. I rued the seriousness of my mistake in 1987, and I constantly replayed the events of those terrible days in my mind. Then, one Sunday morning, an amazing thing happened. My wife Paula, our two sons, and I attended our regular Sunday sermon. Like hundreds of sermons before, I intended to sit in the pew, enjoy the music, listen politely to the words spoken, and go home. However, once the minister, George Mathison, began speaking, my plans changed.

George's words seemed to be aimed directly at me. Suddenly, I was no longer being a passive, polite listener; my attention was focused on every word that George spoke. He was talking about forgiveness and the need we all have to forgive ourselves for the many sins and errors that we have made and will continue to make every day. He talked about the joy that comes from allowing God to share our burdens and the sense of relief that is gained when we realize that we are not carrying the weight of our mistakes alone. George quoted some biblical scripture and summed up his message, "If God can forgive you, surely you can forgive yourself."

I heard that sermon many years ago and I do not remember the exact words spoken, but I will forever remember the essence of the message: Life is difficult on even the best of days. We will make mistakes because we are human and that is the nature of our mortality. However, if we do the best we can, that is all we can expect of ourselves.

George used an analogy that has helped me through the years. He suggested that we all treat our minds like tape recorders with reset buttons. Make the most of each day. Do our best and be the best person we can be. Then, at the end of the day, push the reset button. Do not replay mistakes over and over. Let yourself off the hook. The previous day is gone. Regardless of your wishes, the script of that day cannot be changed or altered. It is written and engraved in stone. Therefore, when the sun rises tomorrow, resolve to begin anew and do the best you can with the new day. Do not waste tomorrow worrying about yesterday.

When I left church that morning, I felt like a heavy load had been lifted from my shoulders. I had truly put my burden down and was able to go through the day living in the present and not the past. I enjoyed that ride home more than any that I have taken before or since. Gradually, with a lot of effort, patience, and persistence, I began applying that same concept that George taught me to my trading. When I made errors, I studied them and worked to change them and do better in the future. But I did not constantly relive them. I let them go and focused on the present and not the past. I began developing a different trading strategy, and central to that strategy was respect for risk. I still traded to make money, but with each order I executed, I considered the risk first. If the risk was too great or if I could not afford the potential loss, I did not take the trade. It was a new approach for me.

In addition to a new respect for risk, I made some other observations. With a clear head that was not burdened by mistakes of the past, I was free to see the markets in a new light. I realized that *time* was a major aspect of trading. In fact, it is one of the only constants in the market. Certain times of the day and of the year tend to be better for my style of trading than other times. Gaining that understanding allowed me to design a strategy around the ideal times for my approach. Hence, time of day became a key element of my trading tactics.

Another characteristic of the market that I carefully watched was *key numbers*. I realized that the market honors or respects some numbers or price points more than others. Therefore, I began studying key numbers, and they are another cornerstone of my trading strategy. I cannot imagine trading without them. I use them to chart my course through the market and determine entry points, exit points, profit targets, and stop/loss placement. Key numbers help me navigate through the market's maze and give me structure.

Finally, I began to watch statistical *market indicators* more carefully. Of course, I had always watched indicators when trading. But now I paid more attention. Remember, I was working to design a strategy that allowed me to trade during the best times for my approach. I also wanted a strategy that considered risk before focusing on profits. I never wanted to repeat the disaster of 1987. If I was going to continue to trade, I needed a plan and strategy that worked for me and my new ideals. After much struggle and effort, I have designed such a strategy. From a disaster, I developed a new attitude and methodology that helps me wage my personal war with the financial markets. That new attitude is summed up in the title of this book: *Trade to Win*.

As each year passes, I realize that I am a rare breed. I have been trading for decades and I am still standing. I have seen a lot of traders come and go. They have a system or a program that works in some specific environments and fails in others. In contrast, my strategy is dynamic and ever evolving. I constantly learn and change. In fact, the students that I have taught over the years have also educated me and because of them my game has gotten better and better. With my strategies, I have the ability to make money in bull or bear markets. I shift and adapt to changes in the world around me. And the environment has definitely changed over the years. Those who did not change with the times were left in the dark. I distinctly remember thinking in 1987 about how wonderful it would be if I had the ability to electronically place orders and hedge my positions via my computer. I envisioned that one day such a thing would be possible, but I had no idea of how such technology would evolve.

When I placed my first trade in the 1970s, I had to maneuver through the streets of Madrid, Spain. It was necessary for me to travel to the office and open my trading account. Once the account was open, I could have phoned orders to my broker, but individuals like me had little information about the daily goings-on of Wall Street. Even traders in the United States, unless they were professionals, did not have access to real-time market quotes. Therefore, the broker was the gatekeeper to the markets. Those seeking information contacted their broker. The broker did the research, made investment recommendations, and placed the trades. After making a trade, it was often days or even longer before verification of the order and the actual price at which the trade was made was known. In those days, the brokerage houses and market professionals controlled everything.

Within the range of my trading career, all of that has changed. When I joined this profession, I did not imagine the transformation that I personally would see and experience. Let me explain the revolution that has taken place in the financial markets with a couple of examples from my trading experiences.

REVOLUTIONS IN TECHNOLOGY AND COMMUNICATION

A sliver of sunlight shone beneath the heavy drapery as I slipped out of my comfortable but small bed a little before 7:00 AM, Paris time. I slowly stepped to the dainty Louis XV desk that sat near the window. Not really my style, but more than adequate space for my trading equipment: my PC was loaded with my trading platform, RoadMap™ software, and real-time market data feed. The Arc de Triomphe stood majestically across the street, but I did not stop to take a peek—I wanted to check on the financial markets. Was some exciting bull or bear action afoot? I turned on my computer and opened my trading programs. The wireless Internet at the four-star Splendid Etoile was working flawlessly and with a few clicks of my computer mouse, I had financial data from around the world at my fingertips. At a glance I determined the general mood of Asian, U.S., and European markets. In particular, I checked the trading price and daily trading range of the Dax futures, a German equity and futures index. That is the index I intended to trade.

I was visiting the Paris Air Show and had business to conduct, but before any appointments were kept, I wanted to make some money. After analyzing the markets for a few minutes, I identified key numbers, checked market indicators, and placed my orders. I traded for an hour or so, located some "low-hanging fruit," and plucked a little for myself. After moving a little of the market's money to my personal financial ledger, I closed my trading platform, and suited up for the other business at hand.

It was June 2007, and I was visiting one of the world's most exciting and beautiful cities. I was a stone's throw from the activity of the Champs Elysées and only a few steps from the Arc de Triomphe, but with modern technology I was able to trade successfully even though I was thousands of miles from my home, my office, and my daily trading routine. Some may say that Paris is for lovers, but for me, Paris is for traders!

Trading is mobile; if a geographic area has the right infrastructure, I can conduct my business—rain or shine, freezing or sultry—anywhere. A few months ago I traveled to Toronto, Canada, where winter is colder than cold. Snow and ice blanketed the city, giving it the look of a winter wonderland. For a southern boy accustomed to warm breezes drifting off the Gulf of Mexico, the weather was almost unbearable. But, in my warm and cozy hotel room, I was able to settle in and do some trading. I was visiting our northern neighbor to attend and speak at the Financial Forum. Because trading is such a huge part of my life, each morning during my stay I traded before heading to the show. I bought and sold both the S&P E-mini and the Dax futures. Moving through cyberspace, I was able to travel around the globe and make money. The Internet allowed me to electronically trade both the Chicago and Frankfurt markets.

On yet another occasion in recent months, I was enjoying the hospitality of the Brits. The cooler temperatures in London made the trip worthwhile. July in Mobile, Alabama, can be oppressively hot, and London offered a brief but pleasant reprieve. But I did not travel across the Atlantic to cool off. I came to attend the Farnborough Air Show. I serve on the Airport Authority in Mobile, and I was attending the show looking for business and opportunities for our city. Again, my hotel was ideal. Standing in sharp contrast to the French décor of the Splendid Etoile, the more contemporary but tasteful rooms at the Hilton Hyde Park offered all the amenities I could possibly need. With Internet capabilities, I easily connected to the financial world and was able to ply my trade. Again, my market of choice was the German Dax. For an hour I sat in my hotel room and did battle with the bulls and bears. As a trader, I was able to travel thousands of miles from home, spend part of my day ferreting out business for my hometown, and still have the capability to trade and make money. Such opportunities were unimaginable to me as a young broker. I was tied to a phone line and the office.

THE DARK AGES: CIRCA 1986

Laura, my personal assistant, and I arrived at the brokerage house early. Once in the door, Laura checked our equipment to be sure that all systems were up and ready to go when the opening bell rang on the exchange floor. That is, she carefully placed pencil and paper on the desk beside the phone. Our other trading tools consisted of a cumbersome data-feed system, a telephone with a dedicated line connected directly to a broker on the trading floor, and a stack of order tickets. Only professionals had access to real-time market data. The trading process was cumbersome, but we did not even realize it. Once Laura or I phoned our orders to the exchange floor, the on-site broker working at the exchange transmitted the order via hand signals to the pit trader for execution. At that time, I considered the speed-dial on my telephone to be a high-tech product. The ability to dial rapidly saved me both time and energy—especially since I placed dozens and dozens of calls to the floor each and every business day. Without the high-tech speed dial, my fingers would have been worn to nubs.

As the minutes passed throughout the day, I executed a barrage of orders. My trading style resembled that of a trigger-happy cowboy practicing his gun-handling skills in the Old West. I traded fast and furious. Just like Earp, I loaded my gun (order slips) and fired all the bullets as rapidly as possible, then reloaded and repeated. I followed the process over and over again. Hopefully, the burst of gunfire hit the target and some of bullets landed directly in the bull's eyes. I was so busy phoning in orders that I had little time for designing a strategy and no time for lunch or coffee. I felt as though I had to schedule time for a bathroom break. When I finally ended my day, my stack of orders stood many inches tall.

When each frantic session finally ended, I did not know for certain whether I had made money or lost it. It could take up to three days to know the fill price for an order. I knew that when I returned to the office in the morning, a stack of confirmation tickets from previous days' trading would be waiting for me. Each order that I had placed would have a confirmation slip in an envelope; the stack of confirmation slips could be a foot high. The tickets verified my fill data. There were no real-time balances available. My monthly account statement would eventually let me know whether my trades had been successful or had missed the target.

In those days, if I traveled for business or pleasure, I did not have the ability to trade. In fact, at home I could not trade. My brokerage office was my only trading center. Trading was the exclusive domain of professionals. That is, individuals had to rely on a brokerage house to handle the ordering process. Odds favored brokers, and those who wanted to play had to enter the market with them and play by their rules and on their turf.

Those who had the greatest market advantage were pit traders. They alone had the ability to place orders quickly and know immediately the price at which those orders were filled. Even as a professional, I had to wait hours or days for confirmations of some of my orders. Clients were even farther removed from the process. They received account information by mail, and the process was slow. In fact, generally all financial communication with clients traveled at a snail-like pace.

Think again about my recent trips to Paris, Toronto, and London. Thousands of miles from home, in a hotel room, I was trading. Technological advances in communication networks made it possible to receive real-time market data around the globe. And those same networks allowed me to view a trading platform, place my orders, and receive almost instantaneous fill data.

The French Revolution may have changed the political paradigm forever, but the communication and technological revolutions have just as dramatically changed the way most of us live and work. Wall Street professionals have seen dramatic changes. And the information and communication revolutions have enabled a new generation of traders to play the financial game. Online brokerage houses, electronic exchanges, and computerized trading platforms allow easy access to the financial markets for the Average Joe. For a small fee, data-feed providers transmit real-time market prices from exchanges in Europe, Asia, and the financial centers of the United States. This data travels to home offices and personal computers sitting in virtually every corner of the United States and across many parts of the world. In the Dark Ages, I relied on my "high-tech" telephone with its speed-dial function. Today, my laptop is the trading equipment that keeps me in touch with the world.

NEW GAMES, NEW TOYS

In addition to ease of execution, computers also allow traders to research companies, products, trading techniques, and strategies. Information is available like never before in the history of mankind. And millions of traders are taking advantage of these new opportunities. I teach trading. I operate a trading school in Mobile, Alabama, and traders from across the United States and some from other continents come to the school to learn the art of trading. Many are retiring and pursuing new careers, others want to learn to manage their own finances or understand how Wall Street operates. Regardless of their motivation, they understand that the market pays for knowledge and new technologies allow them to pursue their dreams.

Instead of a telephone line connected to a trading floor, my equipment consists of computer screens, online trading platforms, real-time data feeds and the equipment needed to transport financial information from around the world to my personal trading center. Color-coded trading software programs analyze and report market data in such a way that in a glance I can determine whether the bulls or the bears are winning the game. With real-time market numbers, I am able to make my trading decisions. I can trade stocks, options, bonds, futures indexes, metals, and energy—pretty much whatever I want. Once my decisions are made, I click my computer mouse and instantly receive my fill. I have the ability to trade at a leisurely pace. When I close my trading platform, I know my profit/loss data. No waiting for hours or days. Each morning I receive an e-mail account statement that verifies the trades I executed and notes my balance.

In addition to the mobility of my trading, my hours of operation have also expanded. Many financial products are traded on electronic exchanges that operate virtually 24 hours a day. Traders are no longer limited to trading only when the pit traders are standing on the exchange floors. Electronic markets and systems expand my trading horizons and allow me to trade virtually any time I choose. Thanks to technology, my world and that of millions of traders has improved. I was able to rise early in Paris and still trade because markets were available. If I so chose, I could have also returned in the evening after a nice meal in one of the city's finest restaurants and still found a market open and ready for business. Within the last few decades, the financial markets have truly undergone a revolution.

Only those able to adapt have survived. I am a survivor because I continuously evaluate the markets and respond to changes. As technology improves, I will also improve and change. Many students who visit my school want a black-and-white trading "system." They want to follow a set of rigid rules and make money. That is not reality. Reality is a dynamic market and the thrill of adjusting and adapting to it. Today, it is easier than ever before to learn about the financial markets and become a player.

BET ON YOURSELF

Without question, investors and traders have opportunities that they have never had before. Like Charlie Prince, the student who showed up in my office a few years ago seeking knowledge about the markets, traders today may choose to personally take the reins of their financial future and determine for themselves where to place investment dollars and how to allocate their assets. The broker or asset manager is no longer a gatekeeper to Wall Street. Sure, a broker is still a vital part of the trading process, but for many traders their broker serves more as their clearinghouse than their market expert or adviser. Millions of traders have online accounts, they do their own research, they make their own decisions, and they place their own trades electronically. Investors have the ability to steer their own financial destiny.

In addition to greater personal control, traders have many more choices. Economically and politically, the world is getting more integrated. China and Asia finance much of America's capitalistic lifestyle. Likewise, American dollars travel abroad seeking investment opportunities and fund much of the development and change in Third World nations. This cross-current of international interdependence increases both opportunities and risks; investing in emerging markets carries unique dangers but may also bring huge paybacks. As the trend toward globalization continues, more opportunities will be available to invest and trade foreign products with ease. On a regular basis, I trade the German Dax futures. If I chose, I could also trade the Nikkei in Japan, the Hang Seng in Hong Kong, or other foreign futures indexes. Some brokerage houses are already offering customers the chance to trade foreign equities—I don't mean via American depositary receipts (ADRs). Mastering the art of 24-hour trading is a must if you hope to achieve consistency with your trading.

Another recent change in trading is the expanded hours of operation available with electronic markets. When I first started trading the S&P futures, my trading day began when the pit traders were ready to go and the opening bell rang. I stopped trading at 3:15 PM CST, when the pit closed for the day. The Globex system operated by the Chicago Mercantile Exchange (and similar computerized trading networks run by other exchanges) have changed all of that. It is no longer necessary to trade only during the day session. Now electronic markets operate virtually around the clock. I often trade at night and enjoy trading in the early morning hours before most traders in Chicago or New York place their first order. Traders may choose to make money during the day, or they may decide to play a game of golf and trade while others sleep.

All of these changes do not come without risk. Those who choose to make their own trading and investing decisions must be able to accept the consequences of those decisions. They need to be educated and informed. Managing your own money and deciding how and where to trade and invest it are awesome tasks. Assuming that job without proper preparation and respect for the dangers involved is foolhardy.

THE CHALLENGE FOR TRADERS

Dealing with dynamic markets and advancing technology is not easy. One has to constantly stay abreast of innovations in both tools and products. No simple "system" will work in every market. In order to win, one must have a winning strategy and execute it properly.

Electronic exchanges, computerized order-entry systems, virtually 24-hour market accessibility—these are only a few of the significant technological changes that have taken place during the last two decades. The expanded hours of operation and easy access to global trading centers allow traders to choose their ideal time and place to trade. My dad, a proud veteran of World War II, was often asked when he had served in the military. His favorite reply was, "I was there when they needed 'em, not just when they were feeding 'em." By that he meant that he served during an active time when things were happening. He was in the real action. He served when the need was greatest. Trading is like that. To make the most money, you must be trading when there is real action. The great ease and market accessibility offered by modern technology allows traders the chance to get into the action and take advantage of powerful market moves around the clock and around the world.

Who knows what will happen in the future? What will trading be like two decades from now? I have no idea, but I do know that those who survive will be the ones who keep up with market modifications, who study, and who adapt to change. Old rules and outdated "systems" do not work now and will not work in the future.

REVIEW

I have been trading for almost three decades. In the life of a trader, that is a very long time. I have seen good days and bad, and I have watched the exchanges and brokerage houses evolve into modern, electronic marketplaces that are so user friendly the Average Joe can trade from his home, office, or hotel room. Furthermore, trading is now mobile, and traders may ply their craft in any geographical area of the world as long as they have access to the Internet.

Over the years I have traded an array of products, including equities, futures, commodities, precious metals, energy and fuels, exchange-traded funds (ETFs), options, and other financial products. In so doing, I have learned a great deal about Wall Street. I know that time, key numbers, and market indicators are important to any successful strategy. I also know that the art of trading consists of mastering many skills. It is necessary to have a strategy that works and to execute that strategy correctly. It is also important to control risk, stay emotionally balanced, and exercise good money management. The remainder of the book will deal with these various aspects of trading.

CHAPTER 2

Time Is Money

In the 1950s, kids didn't sit all day in front of a computer screen or a television set like so many do today. We spent our time outdoors playing ball, riding bikes, or building tree houses. On the corner, just a few steps down from my house, was a large empty lot where the neighborhood boys often gathered to play a game of baseball. It was a ragtag team, and I was one of the younger players. I dreamed of getting a good hit, running the bases, and gaining the respect of my elders. I remember standing at home plate, gripping the bat tightly in my sweaty hands, and waiting for the pitch. Even then, I was well aware of what I needed to do in order to score. I had to concentrate, keep my eyes on the ball, and swing at just the right second. Swing too early or too late and the chance for glory would be lost. Even though I rarely succeeded in my quest, I understood the importance of keeping the ball in focus and swinging at just the right time. For a ball player, timing is not everything, but it is one of the essential elements needed to get a good, solid hit. Timing is also important to trading.

When I placed my first trade nearly three decades ago, trading was also a far different game than it is today. I did not imagine then that in the twenty-first century I would be clicking a computer mouse and making money trading a European or Asian financial product while my neighbors were sleeping. I did not foresee the diverse new products like the equity indexes or the exchange-traded funds (ETFs). In so many ways and in such a short time, the financial markets have evolved and changed.

But, regardless of the changes in technology or products, the basics of trading, like the basics of baseball, remain the same. Winning traders still have to buy or sell at the right price and the right time. They have to make wise and informed trading decisions, and they must have the strategies and the skills necessary to earn money and preserve it long enough to take it to the bank. And, to be a successful trader, you must be able to ply your trade in good times and bad, bull and bear markets.

At the time of this writing, the mortgage crisis is having a dramatic and negative impact on our economy. Consumer confidence is lagging. Oil prices are soaring. The dollar is suffering badly, and many investors and traders are in a quandary as to what to do. The stock markets take a dive one day and rally a few points the next. Unless some factors change quickly, 2008 will not be good for most traders. Many are confused and nervous because they only know how to make money in bull environments. When the bull stops running, they do not have a clue as to what actions to take. However, traders who have the knowledge to trade a variety of products, including options and futures, and those who understand how to trade in bullish and bearish markets can make money regardless of market conditions. This is the best of times for educated traders. Many of those who are educated about the markets are making a fortune. Knowledge will pay.

Luckily for me, over my lengthy trading life, I have seen good times and bad. There have been days when the trading session finally ended and I felt like an old work shirt going through a wringer. I remember the bulky, noisy washing machine my aunt had on her back porch. The clothes washed in a large vat, but in order to finish the job, she had to run them through the wringer and squeeze the excess water out of each garment. On more than a few trading days, those clean clothes and I have had a few things in common—really wrung out. Other days, the market is easy to manage, and when the session comes to a close, I swagger from my desk knowing that I had the knowledge and the skill to make money on Wall Street.

Through those years of experience, I have identified some basic elements of trading that help me survive and prosper. One of the most important elements is time. I divide the 24-hour trading day into four time segments. There is a major market event or events in each segment. These events serve as guides, or at least informational points, along my trading route. Visualize trading around the world and see the whole picture. This will add consistency to your trading. I live in the central time zone. **All times that I use in this book, whether specifically noted or not, are central time.** Please remember that fact when reading all of the strategies and information offered.

Time Segment 1	Asian markets open and lead the way. World traders are looking to the East and the focus is the Nikkei and the Hang Seng.
Time Segment 2	European markets open and exert their influence. If market sentiment is strong in Asia and supported by enough data or emotional fuel, the movement may spread from the exchanges in China, Japan, Singapore, India, and other eastern areas to European shores. During this time segment, Europe leads the way. All eyes are focused on European financial centers and the focus is the CAC (Paris), FTSE (London), Swiss (Zurich), and Dax (Frankfurt).
Time Segment 3	U.S. exchanges open. New York comes to life and trading tends to be fast and furious for 30 minutes or so. Then prices may settle down a bit. However, trading continues to be active for a couple of hours. In the early stages of morning trading, Asia and Europe may influence the mood. If a strong buying or selling sentiment has been expressed, it may gain momentum on Wall Street. Throughout this time segment, U.S. markets dominate the scene. New York and Chicago are alive with trading excitement.
Time Segment 4	The afternoon trading session in the United States may be relatively short, but it may also be important. After lunch and a break from the markets, traders may reverse their morning positions. Or, if they decide they are on the right side of the action, they may add to positions and strengthen the morning move. As in time segment 3, the United States leads the way. The sun is moving westward across the United States, and traders in California and the western United States are weighing in. The trading pits of U.S. exchanges close during this segment.

PEARL 3

The market is open 24 hours a day. Learn how to take advantage of it.

TIME AND ITS IMPORTANCE

If you have any experience trading, you already appreciate the importance of time. Buy a stock on one day or at one time during the day and make money; buy the same stock at the same price at another time or on another day and lose everything. However, nothing etched the importance of that message on my brain more deeply than the crash of 1987. As noted earlier, on that date I was long about 1000 options contracts. I was selling what is called naked options. Arrogantly, I believed the strike price could not be hit and that I would never be called upon to produce the actual products. I was going to mop up the premiums and be fat and happy. My contracts were near expiration when the market headed south. The strike price was hit, and I was forced to ante up. I had to pay a huge price to deliver on my deal and I was busted. I was long at the wrong time. Had I been able to survive for another week, I would have made millions, instead of losing basically everything. My timing (and my disrespect for risk) left me broke. Now I pay attention to time and use time in my trading strategies in several ways.

MAGGIE AND ME

First, I use time to gain insight and knowledge from the time differences around the world. Consider the following event: Bursts of light explode across the sky in Sydney, Australia. It is the dawn of a new year down under. Simultaneously, in my world it is 8:00 AM on New Year's Eve and I am sitting at my desk at home. I watch the celebration taking place on the opposite side of the world on the television screen a few feet away. Maggie, our family bull dog, lies by my feet, keeping me company as I vicariously enjoy the festivities. The Aussies may be ushering in 2008, but I have not closed out 2007. I still have 13 hours to go before I see the sparkling crystal ball fall in Times Square and watch the fireworks burst across the New York skyline. Then it will be another hour before midnight nears and the popping firecrackers disturb Maggie's slumber. If she gets really upset, she might even muster up enough energy to let out a little whimper. The global time difference highlighted by the dawning of the new year is a good example of my first use of time. With the differences in time zones, I am able to preview the trading day—at least preview the day as traders on the other side of the world see it.

The sun moves across the sky from the east to the west, making Asia the first part of the world to welcome each new morning. When Monday's trading session begins in Hong Kong or Tokyo, I am enjoying Sunday evening in the good ole USA. In fact, before I get going on Monday, the Asian trading day is pretty much over. That means that before I execute my first trade, I have the opportunity to know how Asia felt about the financial marketplace. In the land of the rising sun, were they buying or selling? How bullish or bearish were they? Did Asian traders learn of some good or bad news with world-reaching effects? If so, their response to that news will be reflected in the numbers of the Nikkei, Hang Seng, and other exchanges. If there is a price move of 1 percent or greater in the East, maybe the mood will travel westward. Perhaps Europe and the United States will join the consensus and create a wave of buying or selling. If I see a movement forming, I am better able to join it and make money.

Several hours after Asian markets open for business, trading floors in Europe come alive. At 1:00 AM central time in the United States, the German Dax opens. That is, the electronic futures Dax exchange gets going. The Dax cash exchange does not begin trading for another hour when trading floors of major exchanges throughout Europe open for business. Traders begin buying and selling in London, Paris, Geneva, Frankfurt, and all across the continent. Like traders in the East, they are reflecting their view of market conditions. If the financial picture looks rosy, at least for a short time and for their products, they will be bulls. If they see gloom and doom, fear and wisdom will lead them to sell. Again, this buying and selling action has taken place while most Americans are snug in their beds.

Asian markets have closed and European ones are winding down when coffee pots start brewing and eggs scrambling in kitchens across New York and Chicago. However, by then, it is possible to know a great deal about world sentiment. Has some major world event or financial information had an impact on trading to the east of us? Is the world buying or selling in agreement? Sometimes that is the case. On some days, a buying or selling spree begins in Asia and travels across the ocean to Europe. The move gains momentum there and gets even stronger. Then it may continue its surge and travel to the United States. Wise traders who know what has happened around the world have an opportunity to take advantage of the move and use that knowledge and information in their morning trading. Keeping an eye on action across the Atlantic and Pacific adds insight to my trading.

When exchanges open in the United States, trading tends to be fast and furious for an hour or so. Many traders take a peek at prices and jump into the fray. There is an old saying that amateurs open the markets and pros close them. The eagerness of thousands of traders to take on positions shortly after exchanges open creates a surge of activity with generally high volume and volatility in most markets. Personally, I will consider trading until around 10:15 AM central time. Then the volume tends to fall, and activity slows to a crawl. So I, like apparently thousands of other traders, take a break from the action. I do other things and enjoy lunch.

However, after getting a little food in their bellies, many traders return to business. During lunch, they seem to evaluate the morning action. If they agree with the markets' morning moves, they accelerate the pace. A

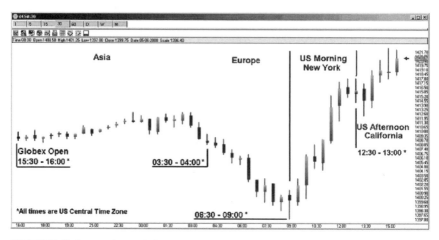

FIGURE 2.1 Tracking global trading from east to west. On weekdays, the Globex electronic trading system opens at 3:30 PM and on Sundays at 5:00 PM. Asia dominates the first time segment. Trading across Europe begins as Asia is winding down. Finally, the sun rises in the United States and our exchanges open in New York and Chicago.

bull market may get stronger as more players go on a buying binge. Or, if a large number of traders decide that things are moving in the wrong direction, a reversal might be in the works. Figure 2.1 is a 30-minute chart of the E-mini futures. Asia dominates trading, as depicted on the left side of the chart. As time passes, trading moves across Europe, and finally the United States dominates the scene.

The important thing to remember is that somewhere around the world financial markets are actively being traded virtually 24 hours a day. The areas of the globe where the sun is shining the brightest tend to be the most active centers. Trading progresses from the East to the West and back again.

Figure 2.2 also depicts this important fact about the use of time. Start at the bottom at the point marked "Market Open." Move clockwise and westward to the Far East. Asian traders exert influence throughout the evening hours. As time progresses, Europe opens; then New York becomes active. Learning and using this concept—that there are four distinct trading setups within a 24-hour time span—will add a level of stability and consistency to your trading.

A great web site for checking market hours is www.marketclock.com. So that is the first way that time is used in my trading strategies. By understanding that trading activity follows the sun, I am able to gain knowledge and insight from traders in Asia and Europe. There are days when that information is not very important. There is no identifiable or profound sentiment expressed. Then there are other days when I am able see a trend

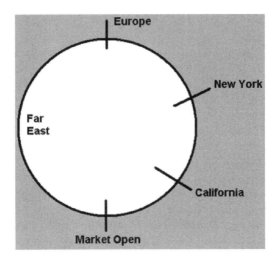

FIGURE 2.2 Wise traders follow the center of trading as it moves from Asia to Europe and then to the United States.

developing. I am able to watch as a buying or selling wave grows in Asia and gains strength as it moves westward. I see the swell get bigger and watch as Europe adds to the move. Then I pay close attention and decide how I am best able to use that information to improve my trading and make money.

TRADING PATTERNS ARE TIMELY

Few things in life are as powerful as habit. In fact, habit is considered to be so powerful that you can actually testify in a court of law about actions that you have habitually taken: like always remembering to click on the turn signal in the car before executing a turn or always following the same route to work. We humans are creatures of habit. We tend to establish certain patterns of behavior and repeat those patterns day in and day out. Traders do the same thing. They do not execute the same trades every day, but they tend to follow the same trading schedule day after day. For example, most traders come to work in the morning, study the markets, determine their strategy and place their trades. Once in the market, they may hold their positions for several hours. As the morning wears on and lunch hour nears, many leave their trading desks or computers and think about lunch. Traders in Chicago, New York, and Kalamazoo all do basically the same thing. They head for the lunch room at the office or café down the street. They enjoy a break from the stress of business and remove themselves from the frenzy of Wall Street. After a nice meal, it's back to business.

I use these trading patterns to help me identify the best times for my trading, especially my day trading. A day trader must have price movement to make money. Why place a trade during the time of day when most traders are having lunch? There will probably be little volume and little to no volatility in prices. Therefore, the trade will be slow to work and the risk of failure is increased. While enjoying their midday meal and stepping away from the fighting on Wall Street, traders evaluate the session. Are prices moving in the right direction? If they agree with the morning's move, they may take on more positions when they get back to the office, and this will accelerate the action. Or are prices going the wrong way? Maybe their morning play was not profitable. In the afternoon, there may be a shift in sentiment. For this reason, I consider the middle of the trading day to be a break in trading, and I reassess my play in the afternoon. Therefore, I use the habits and trading patterns of traders across the United States to identify times throughout the day in the United States when the likelihood of success for day trading is optimal. I use this information to divide my day into three trade zones. During these times I know that, as a rule, the market will give me the volume and volatility that I need to make money quickly. Once I know the best time to trade, I can concentrate on whether to be long, short, or out of the market.

My first trade zone begins when the U.S. exchanges open. The Chicago Mercantile Exchange (CME) and the New York Stock Exchange (NYSE) open at 8:30 AM central time. Once pit traders step into the pits and the opening bell rings, prices start jumping. Traders take on their daily positions, and prices move quickly. Therefore, this is my first trade zone. The rapid movement in prices allows day traders like me to take positions, ride with the market to a quick gain, and exit with profits. The first 30 minutes of trading tend to be pretty frantic, and I do not suggest that the novice trade during this time.

Obviously, if the environment presents chances to make money, it also presents opportunities to lose money and lose it quickly. Therefore, those with little experience should not trade until prices have settled down a bit. The time from 9:00 AM until 10:15 AM tends to generally offer some opportunities for the day trader. After this time, I rarely place a morning trade. Volume leaves the market, and prices stagnate. With that slow movement, risk increases and chances for fast profits diminish. As mid-day approaches in New York and the eastern time zone, trade zone one comes to an end.

My second trade zone begins after lunch. Around 12:30 PM I take a fresh look at prices. Because many traders reevaluate their morning plays and either shift positions or add to existing ones, this can be a good time for my strategy. At least the volume has probably returned to the exchanges and the opportunity to execute a winning trade may be present. Therefore, I look for trading opportunities at this time.

The last trade zone of the day comes when the exchanges are nearing the end of their session. As the day winds down, volume and volatility tend to increase. Some traders realize that they are on the losing team and decide to cut their losses. Other traders are positioning themselves for the late afternoon or evening. Others are simply exiting positions because they are only "day traders" and always move to cash when the pit traders leave the floor. Regardless of the rationale, volatility tends to increase as the trading session draws to an end. Therefore, the time from 2:15 PM until the CME closes at 3:15 PM central time tends to be a good time for day traders in general and for me in particular.

Trade Zone 1	8:30–10:15 AM*
Trade Zone 2	12:30–1:30 AM
Trade Zone 3	2:15–2:45 PM

*All times are central time.

TIME TO STAY OUT

It is important to know when to enter the market, and it is equally important to know when to stay out. In the 1920s, Jesse Livermore, the Great Bear of Wall Street, studied the financial markets extensively. As a young boy, he worked in a brokerage house and continuously wrote down stock prices on a chalkboard. The handwritten chalk prices were traders' version of the current ticker tape. Watching price patterns, Livermore soon understood the significance of timing when making successful trades. Day traders are speculators, not investors. Livermore noted that, "Timing is everything to a speculator." He continued to state the obvious, "It is never 'if' a stock is going to move. It is 'when' a stock is going to move and in which direction—up, down, or sideways" (Jesse Livermore with added materials by Richard Smitten, *How to Trade in Stocks*, Traders Press Inc., 2001). By carefully watching time, I am better able to identify moments that are ripe for profit taking. Richard Smitten recently passed away. I miss talking with him about Jesse Livermore and about trading. Smitten once told me that the basic principles of trading that worked 100 years ago for Livermore still work today. After attending our school, Smitten commented that I brought the theories of Livermore into the twenty-first century.

The winning trader is in the market when the move is taking place and he is on the right side of the action. Trade zones help me identify times when I can anticipate a move and join it to make money.

The flip side of knowing when to get into a trade is having the insight to know when to stay out. Again, according to Richard Smitten, Livermore's biographer, Livermore adamantly believed that no one—regardless of his abilities—could or should trade the markets all the time. There are times when one should be out of the action and on the sidelines (Richard Smitten, *The Amazing Life of Jesse Livermore: The World's Greatest Stock Trader*, Traders Press, Inc., 1999). There are many days when I do not trade. If I do not see the correct setup and I do not believe that the odds of success are in my favor, I do not throw my money away. I wait for a better opportunity to play and win.

Additionally, I have at least one time during each trading day when I will not trade. I will not trade between 1:30 and 2:00 PM. This tends to be a very dangerous time for trading because markets are unpredictable. Experience has taught me that this is a risky time to enter a trade. Prices often just chop around during this time, and it is very difficult to make money. Figure 2.3 depicts the S&P E-mini and the erratic price movements that may be seen during this time. Notice that prices were moving down

FIGURE 2.3 The "Grim Reaper" stepped onto the stage and the downward move of prices halted. As the five-minute chart shows, prices began moving up and down in a very tight range.

uniformly. Then the "Grim Reaper" stepped onto the stage and the trend stopped. The series of short up and down bars on the far right of the chart were formed during the "Grim Reaper" time frame.

If I am in a trade and the "Grim Reaper" is about to begin, I exit the trade and move to the sidelines. It is very rare, indeed, for me to execute a trade or take on a position during this time. I just do not do it because it is so treacherous. Bond pits are about to close, and for some reason this just spooks the market.

One of the biggest mistakes that many traders make is overtrading. Overtrading is the Achilles heel of electronic exchanges. Traders feel that if they are "traders," they must continuously be getting into and out of market positions. Such a view leads to overtrading and losing money. To be a consistently profitable trader, it is necessary to select trading times with care. Only take those trades when market conditions are ideal for the particular strategy being executed. One of the easiest ways to make more money is to stop overtrading.

SPECIAL TIMES TO WATCH

In addition to trade zones, there are some other special times when I enjoy trading. Economic news moves prices. If consumer confidence is exceptionally weak or strong, if consumer prices are rising uncontrollably, if home sales are in the dumps, the financial markets will likely respond. Therefore, I often trade news. I advise novices to stay clear when news reports are scheduled because prices are too unpredictable. However, I have been trading for nearly three decades. I know how to execute trades and get into and out of the market quickly. For experienced traders like me, the news brings the chance to make some quick money. Many regularly scheduled news reports are aired at 7:30 AM or 9:30 AM central time. Sometimes the markets respond quickly and violently to news; at other times, they only yawn sleepily. A later chapter gives some strategic advice for trading news.

The mother of all news events is the Fed. When the Federal Reserve speaks, the markets listen and prices move. At DTI, we love the Fed and use it to make money. Again, strategic advice for trading the Fed is given in Chapter 8.

KNOW WHEN TO CASH OUT

As the Kenny Rogers classic goes, "Know when to hold 'em and know when to fold 'em." Good traders know when to get into the market and when to get out. If a winning position is held too long, it can become a loser.

Prices fluctuate, and at times they fluctuate quickly. When a trade is made, have a profit target or a time limit. When that boundary is reached, exit the trade. Sometimes you may leave a little money on the table, but that is okay. Making money is a good thing, and playing it safe is far better than being foolhardy.

REVIEW

Timing is a critical aspect of successful trading. Execute a trade on one day and make money. Take the same trade a few days later and lose your shirt. Or, for a day trader, go long at 9:00 AM and reap the rewards. Take that same trade at 11:00 AM and live to regret it. Prices move up and down, and making money entails knowing when to take the trade and when to let it go. During my many years of trading, I have identified times when my trading strategies have the greatest odds for success.

By using a global approach to trading, I add insight to my trading decisions. Trading is a 24-hour occupation—at least it can be if one wants to trade around the clock. I do not trade every minute of the day, but I use information from other geographical areas to enlighten my decisions. Centers of active trading follow the path of the sun as it makes its way across the sky from east to west. When folks in the central time zone are at home and relaxing for the evening on Sunday night, the trading pits of exchanges in Asia are alive with activity. Monday's trading day opens and closes in Hong Kong before the first trader ever steps into the pit of the NYSE. European traders also have a chance to place their trades before most traders in the United States make their first play. Before I trade each morning, I check the Hang Seng in Hong Kong and the Nikkei in Tokyo. I also want to know how exchanges in London, Paris, Germany, and Switzerland ended their sessions. Once I have that knowledge, I have a sense of world sentiment. I am then able to use that information and add it to my market analysis.

Over the years, I have noticed how the patterns of most traders affect the markets. When the exchanges open for business, there is a flurry of activity as traders take on their daily positions. The volume and volatility continue for a couple of hours until traders head for lunch. Then there is usually a lull, and prices stagnate for a couple of hours. Once they return to their offices, they add to or reverse their positions and there is usually another flurry of action followed by another lull. Then, as the session draws to an end, volume returns as traders exit the market for the day or cut their losses. Using this information, I trade only during certain times of the day. I have three trade zones when volume and volatility are best for my strategies.

In addition to trading during trade zones, I also trade some news events. Regularly scheduled news moves the markets, and those who know how to use the news make money. I trade many regularly scheduled news releases, including the Fed rate announcements that are scheduled eight times a year. Every Wednesday morning, the U.S. government reports on the status in crude oil inventories. This news is a trader's dream, and I am there ready to take advantage of it. I execute this trade every week live on the web. You have an open invitation to log in and enjoy the show. Go to www.dtitrader.com for the details.

As important as the times when I trade are the times when I stay clear of the markets. One such time is the "Grim Reaper." Each day the time between 1:30 and 2:00 PM is dangerous for me and my strategy. Bond pits are getting ready to close and gauging prices is very difficult. Therefore, I stay clear.

The big idea presented in this chapter is that timing is important to many things in life, and it is especially important to trading. To become a successful trader, pay close attention to time and use it wisely.

CHAPTER 3

Opening the Vault with Key Numbers

S ir Thomas Browne, a noted writer of the seventeenth century, once said that he admired the secret magic of numbers. I do not know exactly what Sir Thomas was referring to several centuries ago, but I agree and I also respect and admire the power and magic of certain numbers. From years of market observation, I know that every financial product has price points, or numbers, that are more important to it than others. These points tend to be price ceilings, floors, and pivots. The interesting fact is that the market remembers these numbers and returns to them over and over again. Therefore, learning about key numbers and knowing how to use them is one of the most important elements in successful trading. I do not believe that anyone can trade to win without using key numbers.

The best way to identify key numbers is through observation. Before trading anything—a stock, bond, future, option, or commodity—watch it trade for a few weeks or months. If that is impractical, pull up some charts and study them. It is a good idea to do both: observe and study. Through observation you learn not only where a stock moved over a given period of time but you have a sense of how it got to that point. You see the up and down bobbles and appreciate how the stock or futures contract travels during specific time intervals. Identify the prices where upward momentum has been halted in the past. How frequently have the bears stepped in at that particular point to push prices back down? If that price point has been hit a number of times and the bulls have been unable to break above it, it is a key number to remember. If the bulls gather enough momentum to break through the price ceiling, they will likely have a nice run to the upside. Of course, the reverse is also true. Identify the price floors. At what points in negative sessions have the bears been stopped? Where are the price bottoms or points of support? Note these numbers. If enough negative sentiment comes into play and the bears are able to force their way through the support level, they will likely move a good bit lower and hit the next support tier.

Therefore, regardless of what you are trading, know the key numbers associated with that product. Especially be aware of the important numbers that are nearest to the current trading price. To execute my strategies, I track and record key numbers and I use them every day. My number-tracking system gives me a long-term, intermediate-term, and short-term market view. I use my RoadMap™ software, and it makes life easier for me. There are other software packages that track the market's action; it is also possible to jot down and follow some numbers manually. However, in this complicated age, there is no substitute for a good computer program for analysis. For serious traders, it is a must.

In order to explain my approach, I have to start on January 1. Each year, I write down the opening prices for each stock, index, commodity, or other product that I plan to trade during the year. The opening price is the single most important number for that product throughout the year. As long as prices stay above the annual open, I will consider a long stock position. However, if a stock price falls below that yearly open, I will not go long until that key price point is broken to the upside. The reverse is also true. That is, the opening price is the line drawn in the sand between the bulls and the bears. A move below the yearly open is evidence of the strength of the bears. Therefore, if prices stay below that all-important annual open, the market has a bearish sentiment. This single tip has saved me a fortune in the current market. At the time of this writing, it is the end of the first quarter of 2008. By respecting the yearly opens, I have no long stock positions. In fact, I am short stocks and have been short. At the time of this writing, the major indexes are down for the year, proving that for the short term my stay-out approach has been successful. Figures 3.1 and 3.2 show the E-mini, mini Dow, and mini Nasdaq drops from the yearly open through the first quarter of 2008. Using this one simple key number and using it effectively has saved me a lot of money.

After I record the open, I continue to track the action from month to month, week to week, and day to day. Each month, I record the monthly opening prices. Are prices moving up or down in relation to the annual open and the previous month's open? Are the bulls or the bears in the most powerful position? As each new week begins, I jot down the weekly open. I continue the process week by week. In this way, I gain a long-term view of the markets. The numbers clearly give me an indication of market sentiment and measure the degree of that sentiment. Therefore, if prices are down for the year, I will hesitate before becoming very bullish. At least with

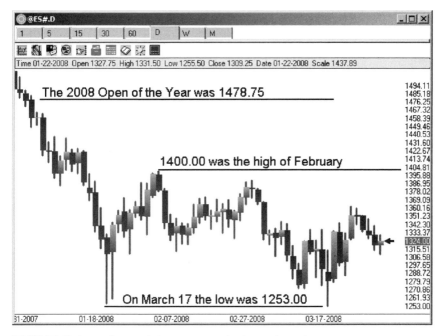

FIGURE 3.1 Evidence of the E-mini S&P's drop. The index lost about 10 percent of value in the first quarter of 2008.

any long-term play. I do not enjoy fighting Wall Street. I want to determine the market's mood and take advantage of trading in the right direction. It is far easier to float with the current as it flows downstream than it is to paddle up a waterfall.

By looking at intramonth data, I am able to gain an intermediate view of the product I am trading. Are prices up or down for the month? If each Monday has seen a lower opening price, I know that a selling opportunity is what I am looking for. Then I just need to determine the best time and the best price at which to sell.

I am a trader. I like to day trade, and I do that often. However, I also make intermediate- and long-term trades. Market conditions determine when and what I do. For my day trading, I enjoy trading futures. I have been trading the S&P 500 equity index futures since their first day of operation in the early 1980s. I also day trade the Dow and Nasdaq futures as well as Dax futures (a German index) and the Dow Jones EuroStoxx (an index listing blue-chip European companies). Therefore, I stay abreast of the key numbers associated with each of these products. I have designed software, my RoadMap™, to automatically track numbers for me and record them for my analysis and review. However, it is possible to keep data manually

(a)

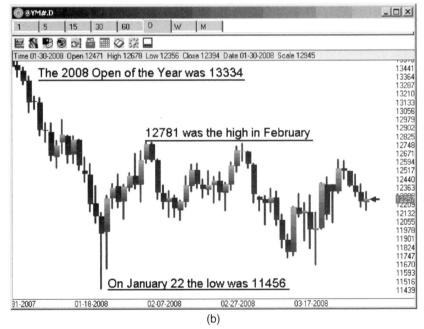

(b)

FIGURE 3.2 (a) The mini Nasdaq drop during the first quarter of 2008. Again, prices fell about 10 percent. (b) Mirrors the move in the mini Dow during the same time frame as Figure 3.2a.

or track them via some other charting software. Winners have some system in place for tracking key numbers.

For a day trader, a short-term view is critical. A day trader is making short-term plays and needs to get it right and get it right quickly. I need to know the key numbers nearest to the current trading price on a daily basis. Each morning, I start by taking note of current key numbers. Where did prices open yesterday? Where did they close? What was the high for the day? The low? What price points or numbers does the market return to over and over again? These are the numbers around which I plan my strategy. Every day, I spend a few minutes before the New York Stock Exchange (NYSE) or the Chicago Mercantile Exchange (CME) opens analyzing key numbers and forming my daily strategy. Never trade without having a long-term, intermediate-term, and short-term picture of the markets in your head. Trading without that knowledge is like throwing a dart across a crowded bar with a blindfold over your eyes. It just makes no sense. You are trading blind.

Once I have identified the level of support (the price floor), the level of resistance (the price ceiling), and pivotal points where prices may reverse, I am able to identify potential buy or sell areas. Never go long just below resistance. Obviously, if the bears come out in force at that price, you do not want to be long and sit foolishly in the line of attack. Wait for resistance to be broken before taking on a long position. Once that happens, the odds are more in your favor that you will be able to ride prices up to the next resistance point. Likewise, do not go short just in front of support. Wait for support to be broken so that you are able to ride prices down to the next support level. That seems very simplistic, but many traders fail to use support and resistance numbers. They buy just before prices tank or sell moments before a rally. That means that they buy the high and sell the low—not what you want to do in most market conditions.

Also remember that there are many key numbers associated with a product. Some key numbers or price points are stronger than others. Again, studying a chart or observing and recording numbers over a period of time should give you the information needed to identify and use key numbers effectively. Once that knowledge is gained, it is a powerful tool for unlocking the secrets of Wall Street.

Opening Prices for 2008

S&P E-mini 500 Futures	1478.75
Mini Nasdaq Futures	2111.25
Mini Dow Futures	13334.00
Dax Futures	8105.50
Apple (APPL)	199.27

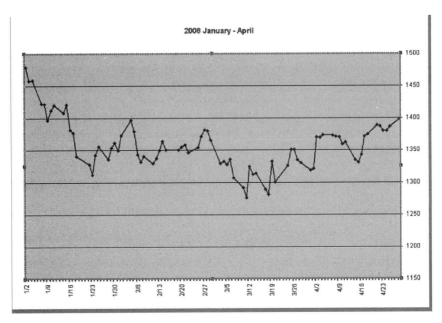

FIGURE 3.3 The chart identifies the weekly opening prices on the S&P E-mini 500 futures from January 1, 2008, through April 23, 2008. The first price charted is the yearly open. As each week begins, the opening price for that week is added to the graph.

I track key numbers on the S&P futures and other futures indexes. Figure 3.3 is a recent trend line of prices on the S&P E-mini futures.

PEARL 4

Record prices on the first day of the year. This helps you trade with the winners.

STOCKS AND KEY NUMBERS

In addition to open and support and resistance numbers, other numbers may also be important. One number that is always powerful is 100. When a stock crosses the $100 mark, there is a strong pull upward to $110. There is something psychological about the zeros—the bulls get energized and move things higher. I learned this lesson painfully years ago when I was short a Merrill Lynch position. I shorted the stock just below the $100 mark. I remember watching Merrill Lynch move up and approach the $100 number. Believing that the $100 price could not be broken, I hung with the trade. Much to my surprise, the $100 was easily crossed, and that Merrill Lynch bull started charging. I was losing money hour by hour but held on, believing that a reversal was minutes away. I was certain that the market would vindicate my play and the price would fall. With each up tick my pain grew more acute. Finally, as the $110 price was in sight, I yelled "uncle," admitted defeat, and closed out my position with a significant loss. When it comes to IBM, Microsoft, Coca-Cola, or any other blue-chip stock, beware of the power of 100. If $100 is broken to the upside, you may want to look to buy. At least, I would not want to go short at that price point and suggest that you not do so. Either stay out of the market or consider a long play. Let me be more to the point—buy at $100 and sell at $110.

PEARL 5

When a stock crosses the $100 price, it will typically go to $110. This also works for stocks crossing the $200 line.

KEY NUMBERS IN METALS, FUELS, AND COMMODITIES

When my first book, *Winning the Day Trading Game,* was published in 2006, crude oil was hovering around the $50 per barrel price. That $50 price was huge and it was a big key number for that particular market. I remember watching that number carefully and planning to buy crude if the $50 mark was broken. As we all know, for a number of reasons crude shot above the $50 mark. Then $100 became the next huge resistance level. It seems like ancient history now but I remember analysts speculating about oil prices and arguing about whether oil could or could not cross that $100 barrier. I take my hat off to T. Boone Pickens. When everyone else was saying that crude had topped out at $50 per barrel and was heading south, Boone alone argued for higher prices. Oil is now trading at record highs. At this time, it is around the $120 area. Can we see $150? As I make money trading crude, I thank T. Boone, the man who leads the charge for the bulls. Figure 3.4 depicts oil's rapid rise across the $100 mark. It is a daily chart for crude futures and shows the meteoric rise of this scarce commodity.

Notice that on March 20, 2008, crude had a low of $98.60. The $100 level served as support for the market and oil held around the $100 level. Unable to move down, it moved back up for a few days and then tested that $100 level yet again. However, within a few days, the bears relinquished control

FIGURE 3.4   A daily chart of crude futures. It captures the $120 high and records rising prices.

and prices took off. At the time of this writing some key numbers for oil as depicted on the chart are the $100 area as well as $110 and $120.

With supplies under stress and demand growing, that $100 resistance level was not too formidable for the bulls. Oil prices escalated to the century mark and soon crossed it. At the time of this writing, crude futures are trading around $120 a barrel. Will we soon see the $150 mark? Only time will tell. At any rate, I would not suggest taking a short or a long oil position during current market conditions until crude falls below the $100 price. Once support at $100 is broken, prices may fall to the $85 mark. In light of current world conditions, it is hard to imagine a huge sell-off in oil. At the present time, the key numbers to watch when trading crude are 85, 100, 110, 120, and 130.

GOLD NUMBERS

Gold is another interesting commodity. Many traders, including me, watch gold prices and use gold as a market indicator. In times of trouble, gold

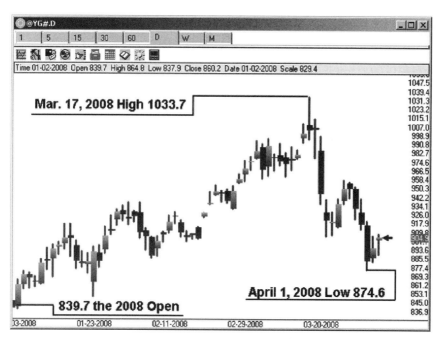

FIGURE 3.5 Daily chart of gold futures for the first quarter of 2008.

and precious metals tend to be a safe haven. Therefore, when gold prices take an upturn, stock prices often move in the opposite direction. The current market is a good example of this phenomenon. At the time of this writing, stocks are down for the year. The housing market is weak and the mortgage crisis is looming. While stocks are down, gold is up. Some of the key numbers to watch when trading this commodity are 1050, 1020, 970, and 950. Remember that the key concept behind key numbers is to buy just above resistance and sell just below support—or at least avoid buying right in front of resistance or selling in front of support. Trade with the market and do not fight it. Identify the trend and ride its wave to profits. Key numbers are moving targets. That is, they change from time to time. Figure 3.5 identifies some of the key numbers for gold in the first quarter of 2008.

When 2008 opened, gold was trading at 839.7. That is a big key number and can be used all year as a benchmark for trading gold. The current yearly high for gold is 1033.7. That number will serve as strong resistance and is another important key number. The low for gold futures when the second quarter of 2008 began was 874.6. This is another point of strong support for gold prices. Let key numbers increase your profits and your consistency.

KEY NUMBERS IN THE EQUITY INDEX FUTURES

I trade futures every day and I could not do so effectively without using key numbers. The yearly, monthly, weekly, and daily opens are important, and I use them to gain a sense of market sentiment and to identify points of entry for trades and profit target areas. I also use key numbers to locate ideal positions for protective stops or stop/loss orders.

When each day begins, I consider prices from the previous day. I want to know yesterday's high and low. I also need the Globex or after-hours trading numbers. Again, I want to know the high and the low. I also consider the 6:00 AM central time Dax price to be an important pivot to gauge the feelings of the indexes. By keeping a watchful eye on these prices I am able to determine at a glance if the bulls or the bears are the most powerful.

Daily Key Numbers to Watch
Yesterday's high
Yesterday's low
Globex high
Globex low
12:30 PM E-mini price
6:00 AM Dax futures price

CONNECTING THE DOTS

I record these numbers for the S&P E-mini 500 futures, the Dow and Nasdaq futures, and the Dax futures. When trading a stock or commodity, I also record the essential highs and lows of the particular stock so that I can gauge the market's mood in relation to that stock. With the help of key numbers, I am able to determine the market's state of mind. The trend comes into focus. By placing the current price into the picture I am often able to get the right direction to win.

"T" SQUARE

One of the exercises that I use to teach beginning traders when to enter a trade is the "T" Square. This is a simple problem-solving method that most college students have learned. I draw a "T" on a piece of paper. On one side of the letter I list all of the reasons for going long at a particular time. On the other side I list all of the reasons for going short. Key numbers are central to my strategy. If the key numbers near the current trading price evidence a move up, the bulls get a check on their side of the "T." When major resistance is broken, the bulls get another check on their side. Or, if the bears are strong enough to hold back the bulls and prevent them from moving above resistance, they earn a check in the bearish column. Using a checklist makes it possible to keep emotions out of trading and focus on the numbers.

The reverse is true for the bears: if support numbers hold, the bulls get the check. The strength of the bears is in question because the bulls succeeded in drawing the line in the sand and defending that price point against attack.

For many years I tracked key numbers manually. Following prices with pencil and paper can be done, but it is time consuming and errors can be made. In this age of Internet communications, there is no need to do it the old-fashioned way. Several years ago, I began working with a software specialist to develop a program that organizes data and tracks key numbers for my students and me. By doing so, the software identifies entry and exit points for stocks, futures, and stock options. I call this particular software my StockBox™. The program cuts many hours off of my preparation and planning time. Figure 3.6 shows the power of technology and how computer programs can analyze and organize masses of data.

StockBox™ records the weekly and monthly high of the particular product being traded. It also notes the average true range (ATR) and the daily open, high, low, and five-day high and low. After noting those key numbers, it identifies a buy and sell zone.

If you want to trade to win, learn about key numbers and use them effectively in your trading. They will serve as guides through the market's maze and help you stay on the right side of the action.

REVIEW

Effective trading requires good analysis of market conditions. One needs to know whether to be long, short, or out of positions. I use time as one part of my analysis, and I use key numbers as another. Without the use of key numbers, I could not possibly answer correctly the long, short, or out question. My trading would be nothing more than aiming at a number on a dartboard.

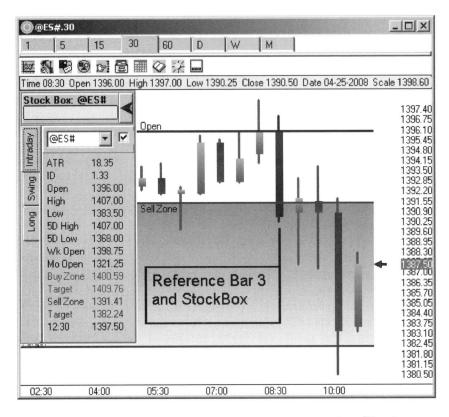

FIGURE 3.6 A 30-minute E-mini chart generated by the StockBox™ software. It tracks key numbers for traders and identifies buy and sell levels.

Every financial product generally has some numbers or prices that are more important than others. The single most important number is the yearly opening price. On the first trading day of each year, record the open. Refer back to this price often and use it as a benchmark to help you determine market sentiment. Are the bulls or the bears up for the year? Once the winning team has been identified, it is possible to decide which side you prefer to join.

Throughout the year I continue to track numbers. I chart the monthly opens and form a trend line with these prices. From that data I am able to gain a long-term view of the mood of the markets. As each week begins, I note the opening prices and put those numbers in the context of my analysis. With each new trading day I record other important numbers. I need to know yesterday's high and low, the high and low made in the after-hours session, the 12:30 PM S&P E-mini price and the 6:00 AM Dax futures price.

By using these numbers correctly, I am able to not only get a sense of the market's possible direction, but I am also able to identify possible points of entry for long or short positions. I am able to hypothesize about potential profit targets for those plays and ponder the ideal placement for stop/loss orders.

For me, key numbers are like hot spots on a map of a mine field. A soldier making his way through that field uses the map to avoid danger and stay on safe terrain. Key numbers are my hot spots. They help me travel through treacherous territory without getting blown up. Consistently profitable traders use key numbers. My goal when trading is to win. Using time of day and key numbers is what puts the odds in my favor. It gives me a structure for trading and helps me keep emotions in check.

CHAPTER 4

Commonsense Market Indicators

"There are lies, damned lies, and statistics." Mark Twain apparently had little regard for the power of mathematical analysis and numerical gauges. In this computer age, it is possible to statistically analyze just about everything relatively quickly. Twain would no doubt be amazed to see all of the information that one is able to obtain with just a click of a computer mouse. There is a chart, curve, diagram, or some other computer-generated graphic for everything. Market analysts track all sorts of numbers and data. There is so much information available that one can easily become overwhelmed. One chart says to buy and another says to sell. One identifies a top and another one points to a continuing trend. Even with so much available, it is difficult to identify indicators that sort through the noise and present helpful information. If one is looking at too many numbers and figures, it is not difficult to become confused. Confusion generates paralysis. It is impossible to know what to do. Like swimming in a sea of swells, it is easy to become overwhelmed and sink in the ocean of data.

For that reason, I have identified some specific indicators that I continuously monitor. In conjunction with time and key numbers, I use these indicators to find my way through the labyrinth of Wall Street. Experience has taught me that if I keep my eye on these indicators, I am able to put the odds of success in my favor. The first indicators that I monitor are the futures indexes. Specifically, I track seven of these and refer to them as the Seven Sisters. They are the S&P 50-mini futures, Nasdaq 100 futures, Dow 30 futures, Dax futures, gold and oil futures, and bond futures. I generally track the mini contracts on each of these.

52   A FOUNDATION FOR SUCCESS

Seven Sisters

1. S&P 500 futures (ES)
2. Dow 30 futures (YM)
3. Nasdaq 100 futures (NQ)
4. Dax futures (FDAX)
5. Gold futures (GL)
6. Oil futures (CL)
7. Bond futures (US)

I keep track of the futures indexes because I consider them to be a good reflection of the aggregate attitudes of traders about the overall condition of the markets and the prospects for the future. It is my belief that futures contracts are market leaders and will guide me in the right direction. Tracking the Seven Sisters is a simple way to organize data and get a worldview. Of course, I also trade these products.

In addition to the futures equity indexes, I keep an eye on gold, oil, and bond futures. I watch gold because it plays a unique role in the markets. Gold is an international currency. When traders and investors around the globe fear that inflation is eating away the value of their cash or stock portfolio, they frequently look to gold. Also, historically, gold has been viewed as a safe haven in times of turmoil and crisis. Because emotion plays such a big role in investing and trading, when market participants become fearful, they flock to gold and precious metals for security. If gold sharply rises, it means that traders have lost faith in other investments and are plowing cash into precious metals. That is, the confidence level of investors is being undercut. When this occurs, the U.S. dollar is also likely to be weak. Therefore, during times when gold is moving up, stocks are often moving down. For all of those reasons, I watch the price of gold and use it as an inverse indicator. Gold and precious metals add another dimension of analysis to my trading decisions. Additionally, I also trade gold.

Another commodity that I track, especially in this market, is oil. Oil is vital for the growth and continued functioning of our economy and our way of life. In fact, the United States is the world's biggest consumer of oil. However, China is becoming another huge petroleum market. When oil prices rise too high, the entire economy feels the pinch because it becomes costlier to produce goods and to transport them. When consumers have to pay more at the pump, cash is siphoned from the economy and there is less to spend for consumer goods like automobiles, clothes, and houses. With so much turmoil in the Middle East and in other oil-producing areas, prices may jump quickly when supplies are threatened. As a rule, when oil prices are deemed to reach a point where they are costing the economy too much, stock prices will fall. In 2007 and 2008, oil has been reaching historic highs. With China racing toward industrialization, there seems to be no end in sight for continued stress on oil and energy. Under current market conditions, oil is also one of my trading favorites.

TRACKING THE SEVEN SISTERS

I begin my analysis at the first of each year. I track the opening price for each of the Seven Sisters. When they come out of the chute on the annual opening day of trading, at what price do they debut? As the hours, days, weeks, and months continue, how will each index trade in relation to their open? If prices stay above the open, I will look to the bullish side for the long term. If they are below the open, I will be considering a short—at least for long-term analysis. I continue my tracking process and as each month begins, I record the monthly opening price and compare that price to the yearly open and to the previous monthly opens. I want to know if prices are trending up or down.

I use a telescopic approach and focus my attention on smaller and smaller time frames. As each week begins, I add that number to my analysis. In relation to the yearly and month opening prices, should I be bullish or bearish? In comparison to the previous week's action, are prices higher or lower with each weekly open? To gain a perspective of the current market, I look at daily prices intraweek. When each day begins, I note the opening prices and place those prices in the context of my yearly, monthly, and weekly analysis. On this particular day, where are prices? Are they following an established trend? If so, what is that trend? If not, for how long have prices been reversing? All of this information gives me insight into the sentiment of traders and helps me determine the action that I should be taking.

Each day, I focus on several important times and take note of how the Seven Sisters trade during these times. I label the price bars formed during these significant 30-minute time frames as reference bars. The name reflects the role these prices play in my trading strategy. As I trade I continuously refer back to the highs and the lows of these price bars to determine entry and exit points as well as profit targets and stop/loss placement. These reference bars help guide me through my trading day. The four times that I always watch are 3:30 to 4:00 PM (my reference bar number 1 time frame), 3:30 to 4:00 AM (my reference bar number 2 time frame), 8:30 to 9:00 AM (my reference bar number 3 time frame), and 12:30 to 1:00 PM (my reference bar number 4 time frame). When I say that I "watch" prices during these times of day, I do not mean that I sit in front of my computer screen and manually record prices. In this electronic age, computers will do the work for you, and I let mine gather numbers for me. With my RoadMap™ software I track prices every 30 minutes. The prices are recorded and I am able to refer back to them as the need arises. There are other software packages that may be purchased that can track and analyze data for you. Find one and use it.

Once the numbers are obtained, I record the high and the low of trading during these 30-minute time spans. I refer to these 30-minute bars as reference bars because I use these prices as reference points for my trading. I refer back to them throughout my trading day for guidance.

I selected these times based on the global financial markets and important events that occur at various times. At 3:30 PM the Globex or after-hours electronic system comes online and traders from around the world begin making their after-hours plays. For that reason, I deem the first 30 minutes of trading to be important. The second price bar that I use for reference is formed between 3:30 and 4:00 AM. At that time, Asian exchanges have closed and European exchanges are going full speed. By taking a slice of that price action, I am able to get an idea about how Europe views the markets. A short time later, New York and Chicago come to life and the NYSE, CME, and other large exchanges open their trading floors. The eyes of the world focus on the United States, and our financial markets lead the way in world trading. As the sun moves westward, traders across the nation take a break from trading and enjoy a midday meal. After returning to their trading platforms, they rethink the morning's action. Do they agree with the day's move or do they want to shift gears and join the other side of the action? In the afternoon, prices may reverse or accelerate a move begun in the morning. For that reason, I use the 12:30 to 1:00 PM price bar for orientation for afternoon trading.

In Chapter 2, I explained how I divide my analysis into time segments. Asia dominates the first time segment that extends from 3:30 PM until 3:30 AM. During this time segment, I rely heavily on the price bar that is formed between 3:30 and 4:00 PM and the action in Asia. If prices move above the high of that Globex opening price bar or reference bar and the move is confirmed by rising prices in Japan and China, I look to go long. If prices move below the low of that bar, with confirmation from the East, I look to the short side. I may also consider some other factors, but the reference bar and the mood across the Pacific are a big part of my analysis.

Likewise in time segment 3, I use the first 30 minutes of trading between 8:30 and 9:00 AM to guide me. In the United States, the open outcry pits have opened and traders are positioning themselves in the markets. As trading continues throughout the day, I constantly refer back to both the opening price and the opening price bar to gain a perspective and determine how I want to play. Are the bulls or the bears leading the daily game? I want to play on the winning team. Figure 4.1 is a reference bar chart for

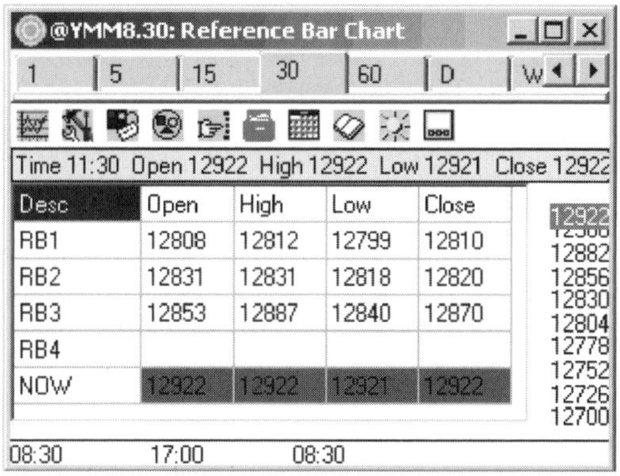

FIGURE 4.1 Example of the reference bars that I use to guide my day-trading path. These reference bars identify the high and low during a specific 30-minute time frame.

the E-mini futures. The important information that I need to know is the opening price, closing price, high, and low during a specific time of day.

Therefore, the Seven Sisters are important to my trading and I use them as indicators of market sentiment. They point me in the right direction. If there is divergence among the Seven Sisters, I stay out of the market. For example, there are days when the Nasdaq index is trading in positive territory while the S&P or Dow is posting negative numbers. Such divergence signals danger. The message is one of confusion. Traders in general are unsure as to what action to take. There is no market consensus. On these days it is impossible to put the odds in my favor. Therefore, I sit and wait and keep my powder dry. There will be better days when the direction is clear and the odds for success greater. I will patiently wait for those days.

In addition to these guides, I use some other statistical indicators. I generally keep an eye on the New York Stock Exchange (NYSE) and Nasdaq issues, the NYSE tick, the Arms Index, and a couple of indicators that I have designed.

THE NYSE AND NASDAQ ISSUES

The NYSE and Nasdaq issues reflect the number of stocks that are above their previous day's closing price as compared to the number that are below that price on the NYSE and Nasdaq 100, respectively. These statistical indicators are important to my trading approach. When gauging them, I use 500 as a benchmark or watershed level. If 500 or more of the issues are trading above their latest closing price, I will look more to the bullish side. If

500 or more of the issues are negative when compared with their previous day's close, unless there is some other strong information to the contrary, I will be looking for a shorting opportunity. If both the NYSE issues and the Nasdaq issues are strongly expressing a bullish or a bearish opinion, I pay attention.

I never trade without taking a look at issues. Sometimes the NYSE issues will be moving in one direction and the Nasdaq issues will be trending in another. Such divergence is a red flag and I keep my hand off the mouse. When two major indexes or indicators are moving in opposing directions, it tells me that traders are confused and no trend has been identified. When I see that scenario, I move to the sidelines and wait for a discernible trend to appear.

The NYSE issues may be used only during the hours that the exchange is open. Therefore, other indicators must be used after hours. However, if the issues were very opinioned at the close, they may point the way toward a direction for trading the night markets. For example, if the issues are positive 1500 at the session's close, traders have expressed a bullish mood and one would need to exercise care and caution before taking a short position in the night market. If going short, be sure there is confirmation of the move from some other benchmark.

THE NYSE TICK

Another indicator that is followed by many traders including myself is the NYSE tick. This indicator reflects the difference between the number of stocks ticking down and the number of stocks ticking up in price on the NYSE. This is a leading indicator for market direction. It is like the rpm gauge of Wall Street. If this indicator is strongly positive, start looking for a buy point; if it is strongly negative, you do not want to join the bulls. If you trade with a strongly negative tick, you will likely be a seller. Readings that are +500 to −500 are neutral and I do not deem them to express any specific sentiment. However, once readings register more than 500, I believe a sentiment is evident. The higher the number soars, the stronger the sentiment being expressed. If the tick reaches 1000 plus or minus, the mood of the market is undeniable. When prices go so high, the market is probably overbought or oversold, and a reversal—even if small and brief—is to be expected. When the markets are running so fast and furious, they simply need to breathe and may take a rest. A tick reading of 1000 simply cannot be maintained for very long, at least not on the average trading day. If the market is indeed bullish, after taking a brief rest, prices may surge again.

Therefore, if the NYSE tick is measuring 1000 and I am looking to go long, I will probably wait until the tick backs away from the high before executing my trade. Then, if conditions support a long position, I may buy the pullback. If I buy when the tick is so hot, I may be buying at the top—not a position I want to be in.

Although I consider the NYSE tick to be important, it is only one of the indicators that I track. I view the tick data in conjunction with the Seven Sisters and the other indicators discussed in this section.

Like the NYSE issues, this indicator functions only when the NYSE is actively trading. It cannot be used during the evening or night for guidance. However, like the issues, at times the market's mood will be so strong that the indicator can be used to judge general market sentiment.

THE TRIN

The TRIN, also known as the Arms Index or Trading Index, measures volume and the previous day's close. The TRIN is a ratio of ratios. It is calculated as follows:

$$\frac{\text{Advancing Issues/Declining Issues}}{\text{Advancing Volume/Declining Volume}}$$

The TRIN is a contrary indicator. That is, the more positive the reading, the more negative the market's sentiment. A TRIN of 1 is considered neutral. That is, there are about as many buyers as sellers. As the NYSE Tick moves up, the TRIN moves down. The TRIN may go as high as 3.5 or as low as 0.30. Between 1.20 and 0.80 tends to be a noise zone in which no direction is indicated. When watching the TRIN, look at relative price action and not absolute value. For example, if the TRIN is 1.5 and it moves to 1.2, the direction is bullish even though the absolute value is slightly bearish.

Again, I consider this indicator in relation to the other indicators that I monitor. I never make a trading decision on the basis of the TRIN alone. It is part of my overall analysis. It is one piece of a larger puzzle. There have been occasions when the TRIN has saved me from making a big mistake. Some of the other indicators were pointing in one direction, but the TRIN was giving a contrary message. I hesitated to act in haste and the TRIN's warnings saved the day.

THE V-FACTOR AND THE TTICK

In addition to the indicators used by most traders, I also have two proprietary indicators that I created. One of them gauges momentum and one volume. The V-Factor tracks momentum as traders enter the market. Most experienced traders use volume data in some manner when they trade.

Generally, if a trend is strong, it will intensify as volume increases. Likewise, as volume wanes, it may be time to exit the market because without momentum, money cannot be made as easily.

The V-Factor records the volume and identifies the number of buyers and sellers. Then, the ratio is expressed in an easy to read format. The V-Factor can be reset during critical times during the day to check the current volume and the bias of the majority of traders during any trade zone or significant time frame.

Here is how the V-Factor works: If the V-Factor is 1.0, there are an equal number of buyers and sellers. If the V-Factor is 0.05, there are twice as many sellers as buyers. If the V-Factor is 2.0, there are twice as many buyers as sellers. I watch the V-factor while I am trading. If I am long in the market and the V-Factor indicates that a great deal of selling has stepped in, I may seriously consider exiting my position or lightening it. Use the strategy or program that you like, but if you expect to be a winner, watch volume.

Figure 4.2 is a V-Factor reading. The V-Factor graphically depicts volume in three formats. Comically, the dominant side is pictured as either a bull or a bear. In Figure 4.2, the bears are roaming, and it might not be a good time to go long. Also, the concept is conveyed with a bar graph. The higher bar on the right shows that the bears are slightly greater in number. Finally, a chart plots the strength of the bulls and the bears. The line on the top shows the bears with greater volume than the bulls.

Another one of my personal indicators is the TTICK. I created this indicator several years ago, and I use it every day. The TTICK combines

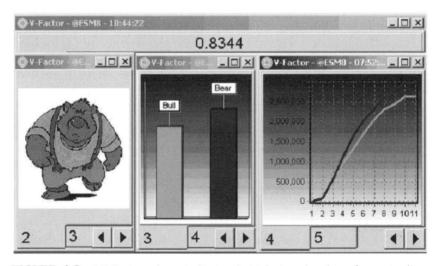

FIGURE 4.2 A V-Factor volume indicator that I designed and use for my trading.

information from the S&P futures and the NYSE tick and synthesizes it and smooths it out. The TTICK readings run from +30 to –30. A reading of 10 is deemed to be noteworthy; +10 is strongly bullish, and –10 is strongly bearish. When readings approach 20—either plus or minus—prices are probably reaching an overbought or oversold condition and there may be a brief rest in the move. Under certain market conditions, I rely heavily on this indicator and consider it in the context of the total market. For me, the TTICK is another weapon in my arsenal.

There are times when the TTICK is positive and the NYSE tick is negative. That is a clear message to stay away from my mouse and out of the market. The TTICK has helped me many times, and if in doubt about a trade, I look to the TTICK for guidance. Among the indicators, it is often my ultimate judge.

REVIEW

Computers allow for many calculations to be made very quickly. Therefore, modern traders have the ability to obtain statistical analyses about almost anything. Such easy access to information is a double-edged sword. Information is good, but too much information can be unsettling and lead to the inability to see a trade and make a decision. While you are analyzing the data, the trade comes and goes without an entry. Therefore, I use a few pieces of data to help me see through the market maze. I rely heavily on the futures indexes, including the S&P, Nasdaq, Dow, Dax, gold, oil, and bonds. I refer to these indexes as the Seven Sisters. When trading, I want these indicators to agree with one another and be moving in the same direction. If all of them are moving up, I will likely be considering a long position. I certainly will not be going short. If they are trending down, a short will be my play. However, if even one of these futures indexes disagrees with the others, I will stay out. Divergence is a sign of caution, and wise traders will heed it.

I also track the NYSE issues, the Nasdaq issues, the NYSE tick, and the TRIN or Arms Index. In addition to this information, I have devised two proprietary indicators: the TTICK and the V-Factor. These gauges measure momentum and volume and help me stay on the right side of the action.

Time, key numbers, and the statistical indicators noted in this chapter are my market filters. Using these market fundamentals keeps me on the winning side of the action most of the time.

PEARL 6

Do not worry about the direction the market goes. Go with the market.

CHAPTER 5

The Art of Trading

"Nothing endures but change." When ancient Greece thrived, Heraclitus developed his philosophies about the universe and the central role of change to it. He understood that change is one aspect of life that is predictable and certain. That is, over time nothing earthly remains the same. The rule clearly applies to financial markets. They are dynamic and challenging. Every day brings new developments and new difficulties. Bull and bear markets come and go, and successful traders must accept that reality and deal with it effectively.

Trading is an art and not a science—that is why it is so challenging and downright difficult. Winning traders must constantly measure, gauge, compare, and evaluate. The financial markets are vibrant. By their very nature they are continuously in a state of flux. Therefore, winning traders must adapt and change with them. Winners must also continue to educate themselves and learn new strategies, new techniques, and new approaches. There is no simple rule to follow or program to execute that will always return a profit. Many traders look for a system or a program that will take the risk out of trading. If you don't already know, let me be the first one to tell you that those systems do not work. They may do well in a bull market, but when consumers lose confidence in the economy and stock prices fall, the system is no longer effective. Or they may do well in some sectors, but may not work if applied to others. No system has the ability to analyze and react to markets that are always rising and falling and affected by an array of economic and political factors.

TIME

The art of trading involves properly reading the tape. In Chapters 2, 3, and 4, I discussed the fundamentals of successful trading. The first fundamental is time. One has to trade at the right time of day, week, or month to make money. Every trader has executed a trade at just the wrong time. For example, he has bought the top or sold the bottom. That same trade executed at a different time would have resulted in profits, but the timing of the trade was off and there was a loss. In trading, timing is not everything, but it is extremely important.

Day traders must have volatility and volume to trade. If there is no volatility, prices are flat. A trade is made and the price does not move. Obviously, if there is no price movement, there is no opportunity to make a profit. Volume translates into liquidity. Traders not only need to get into the market, but they also need to be able to get out of it when they so choose. If there is no volume, there are not enough buyers and sellers to allow for the ease of ideal entry and exit. Chapter 2 deals with the best times for executing my strategies. I do not trade stocks or any other financial product that is not liquid. When trading stocks, I trade only those with 2 million or more shares traded, on average, in any trading day. The S&P, Dow, Dax, and Nasdaq equity indexes are all highly liquid products to trade, and my method identifies the best times of day for me to trade them.

KEY NUMBERS

The second fundamental of trading is key numbers. I use key numbers to find my way through the market's noise. Key numbers are for me like a buoy is to a ship's captain. They mark off places where danger lurks so that I can avoid disaster. Skilled tape readers know support and resistance levels identified through the use of key numbers. That information helps them avoid buying tops and selling bottoms. It gives them the ability to identify ideal entry prices and establish profit targets. It also is beneficial in finding the right location for a stop/loss order. Mastering key numbers is another big part of proper tape reading.

MARKET INDICATORS

A third fundamental of good trading is the proper interpretation of market indicators. Traders need gauges to maneuver through the maze of prices and data. Tracking statistical data is an important part of that process.

Watch the Seven Sisters described in Chapter 4. Before placing a trade, see what the Seven Sisters are telling you. Are they moving up or down? Are they in agreement with each other, or is there a difference of opinion among them? If there is divergence among the indexes, the signal is clear. The market is confused as to direction and wise traders stay out. However, if the S&P, Nasdaq, Dax, and Dow are all trending in the same direction, perhaps it is time to take a closer look at prices. Then take a glance at the other indicators. How is gold trading? Is oil moving up or down? What about bonds? Are all of the Seven Sisters in agreement with a long or a short position? If so, look a little closer.

Check the statistical indicators. Is the NYSE tick registering a market view worth noting? That is, is this statistical indicator reflecting a bullish or a bearish sentiment? Look at the issues. On the NYSE and the Nasdaq, how are issues doing? Are prices up from yesterday or are they down? If they are expressing a strong sentiment, what is that sentiment? Do these indicators agree with the Seven Sisters and each other?

Next, take a glance at the Arms Index or the TRIN. Is the TRIN supporting a buy or a sell? Or it is signaling caution? Finally, I look at my personal indicators—the TTICK and the V-Factor. What are these numbers telling me? Before I trade, I evaluate the whole picture. Is there a consistent message, or is the market confused? If it is confused, I stay out. But if there is a clear mood expressed, I look for a point to execute a trade.

Is the time right? If not, wait. If so, consider key numbers. What key numbers are near the current trading price? Is the market near a strong point of resistance? If I am going long, I will wait for resistance to be broken before making a play. Where is support? If I am going short, I will patiently wait until support has been broken. Then I will ride the move down to rake in some profits.

The big point here is that all of the fundamentals of trading must work together. Trading at the wrong time will not lead to success. Improperly interpreting indicators or reading them at the wrong time will not lead to victory. Merging the elements of trading and using them in the proper way and at the proper time will produce a winner. Like creating a piece of art, there are many decisions, nuances, angles, and the like that must be considered. Trading is not easy, and few put forth the effort to educate themselves and master the skills to win the game.

THE FOURTH ELEMENT

Unfortunately, the analytical aspects are only part of the picture. The artistry of trading also involves emotional balance and good risk management. Winning traders must learn to keep their emotions in check and trade the numbers, not their hopes, dreams, or fears. Even with the best analysis, when emotions get in the way, money will be lost. Part Three of this book deals with the nonanalytical parts of trading. It is these factors that are the most difficult to master. I have seen many "wannabe" traders who think that they can learn a one, two, three-step approach to trading. Unfortunately, trading is far more complex than that. Having a high IQ does not translate into being a good trader. It may help with analysis, but if you are unable to balance fear and greed or if you cannot accept the fact that you can and will make mistakes, you will not be successful. The financial markets have a way of keeping even the best of us humble.

When money is on the line, a winner has to be able to keep a cool head while properly reading the indicators and making good decisions—not emotionally charged ones. Winners must respect risk and manage their money. The right combination of intellect and emotional stability is essential, and there is no substitute for experience. In addition, you have to have enough capital to play the game. As the old adage goes, it takes money to make money. For that reason, risk management is decisive. Knowing when to hold 'em and when to fold 'em is a critical aspect of trading. For all of these reasons, I speak of the art of trading.

The Steps to Win

I. Evaluate the Seven Sisters
   1. S&P 500 futures
   2. Nasdaq 100 futures
   3. Dow 30 futures
   4. Dax futures
   5. Gold futures
   6. Oil futures
   7. Bonds
II. Gather Important Numbers
   1. Yearly opens
   2. Monthly opens
   3. Weekly opens
   4. Daily opens
   5. Bars of reference (high and low in the following 30-minute time frames):
      3:30–4:00 PM
      3:30–4:00 AM
      8:30–9:00 AM
      12:30–1:00 PM

III. Check the Economic Calendar
  1. Record important news items.
  2. Look at a 24-hour trading day.
  3. List each important news event by date and time.
  4. Be ready to make money when the time comes.
IV. Execute a Winning Strategy
  Once market direction has been determined, the following strategies are possible:

  Buy stock or futures.
  Buy calls.
  Sell puts.

  Sell stock or futures.
  Sell calls.
  Buy puts.

V. If No Direction Can Be Identified—STAY OUT OF THE MARKET!

REVIEW

Formulas work in laboratories and classrooms, but they do not work when one is trading the financial markets. Markets are dynamic, and prices are continuously shifting and changing. Only traders who know how to read the tape will survive. Those traders possess many skills. They understand the importance of time and utilize it effectively; they comprehend the power of key numbers and exploit them successfully; they use reliable market indicators to cut through the market maze and identify the sentiment of traders and thereby pinpoint the direction of prices. In addition, they have emotional balance and use good money management and risk aversion techniques. Trading is an art, and through education and experience the artist will become more skillful at executing his craft. He will learn to trade when the odds of success are on his side and stay out of the market if the setup is not right.

PEARL 7

Chicken, fish, or steak? Make a decision and move on it.

PART TWO

Strategies to Win

CHAPTER 6

The Path of Least Resistance

I t was 1982 and I was working for a large brokerage firm in Oklahoma City. I had anticipated this day for weeks. The Chicago Mercantile Exchange (CME) was finally launching its new product, the S&P 500 index futures. I had been reading about this new kid on the block for some time, and now it was finally my turn to play. The overall market was bullish. The major indexes were looking healthy and moving up steadily. I knew the excitement that surrounded this new CME trading venue, and I suspected that prices would move up quickly once it was off and running. Therefore, on my first day of trading, I joined the bulls. I remember little else about the day except that I went long and I made money. My first experience with the S&P futures was a positive and exciting one. From that moment on, I was hooked on trading the equity index futures.

Since that time, I have traded it literally thousands of times. I enjoy buying and selling the S&P for several reasons. First, I like the leverage. It is possible to trade the S&P futures, Dow futures, and Nasdaq futures with a relatively small account balance. Many brokerage firms allow you to trade one mini futures contract for as little as $2500 per contract. Some brokerage houses require even less. At the time of this writing, the mini-S&P is trading in the $1400 range. There are four ticks to a point and the value of each point is $50. That means that each small or mini S&P contract controls approximately $70,000 of market value. Yet, one can control that contract with as little as $2500 of good-faith cash in his account. Because I am an experienced and knowledgeable trader, the leverage works well for me and allows me to get a huge bang for my bucks. The payback can be highly lucrative. I trade the S&P, Dow, Nasdaq, and also the Dax and

Euro-stock equity index futures. One must have a margin account to trade futures. A regular stock trading account cannot be used.

The leverage that works well for me can be disastrous for a trader who does not understand the market. He will lose money and lose it fast. In fact, one of the downsides of futures is that you can lose more cash than you have in your account. As with any margined trading account, you must maintain a minimum balance to support your level of trading. If funds fall below that level, a margin call will be issued. That means that the monetary shortage must be immediately covered or some really bad things can happen. Therefore, before you trade futures, know and understand the risk and be certain that you can afford those risks. Also, educate yourself before you trade. In addition to learning the ropes, observe trading for some time. Get a feel for how prices move and spend many hours engaged in simulations.

Anytime money can be made quickly, it can also be lost in the blink of an eye. Therefore, when you are trading futures, it is critical that you know and use good money management and risk management skills. Use protective stops and other money management strategies explained later in this book.

Another great aspect about trading futures is that it is possible to make money in bull or bear markets. In fact, in a bear environment, when prices begin falling, they tend to move downward much more quickly than prices move up in a bullish environment. When prices move up, they usually move up in steps and then consolidate. In contrast, once prices start plummeting, they often just race down. Therefore, the flexibility and possibilities of trading futures are very alluring to me.

There is rarely a business day when I do not trade index futures. I have many strategies for various market conditions. However, I have selected an S&P, a Nasdaq, and a Dow breakout trade that I have been making frequently in current market conditions. When I refer to a "breakout" trade, I mean that for some reason prices move out of an identified range and break above or below it. Sometimes news will move prices up or down, or a price movement may be generally associated with a time of day, month, or year. At any rate, these trades are made when the breakout occurs. Let's begin with an S&P trade. The following trades are day trades, not investments or long-term positions, and they are made in the futures markets.

THE FACE PEEL

I call this trade the "Face Peel" because if you are unfortunate enough to get caught on the wrong side of it, you will feel the pain of a peel. It is an

S&P 500 trade. The S&P 500 is traded at the CME. There are two contracts: the big contract trades for $250 per point, and the mini contract trades for $50 per point. The mini contract has 4 ticks to a point, and the big contract has 10 ticks per point. The S&P can be traded virtually around the clock. The open outcry pits of the CME open each day at 8:30 AM central time. The big contract is traded via the pits from their opening until the pits close at 3:15 PM. Then trading shifts to the electronic platform or Globex. The mini S&P is always traded electronically on the Globex. This virtual trading arena opens for business each afternoon and continues for almost 24 hours. On Sundays the Globex opens at 5:00 PM, and on Monday through Thursday it opens at 3:30 PM. Like the trading pits at the CME, the Globex closes its session at 3:15 PM the following day.

The Face Peel is executed near the end of the session as the CME approaches its 3:15 PM close. I consider this trade only if the overall markets, including the S&P 500, have made a pronounced move in one direction or another during the session. I have no magic number of points of movement to signal such a move. It is similar to the view of Supreme Court Justice Potter Stewart in 1964 speaking about pornography: it is difficult to define but "you know it when you see it." When you experience a day of pronounced market movement in either direction, you know it. As the session nears its close, prices are notably up or down from their opens and they have been trending in the same direction throughout most of the day. This directional movement signals the possibility of a Face Peel.

On days when such a move occurs, this strategy may be a good play. Many times, a market that has been opinionated throughout the day will make a correction at the close. However, if the opposing team makes a failed attempt to shift directions but cannot cross the 2:30 PM price, the day's earlier move is often accelerated. To gauge this possibility, I record the 2:30 PM S&P price. Then I monitor prices for about 15 minutes. If there is going to be a reversal or correction, the 2:30 PM price should be broken to the upside or downside, depending on the direction of correction. Therefore, around 2:45 PM, I again record the price and compare it to the 2:30 PM price. If the downtrodden side has been unable to break the 2:30 PM price, I trade in the direction of the trend. That is, the opposing side is too weak to rally so the trend of the day should continue and accelerate to the close.

I execute the trade and ride with it until 3:14 PM or so. However, prior to 3:15 PM, I close out the position. I do not hold futures contracts from session to session. Doing so results in a much higher margin requirement. If I want to trade the after-hours market, I reenter after the Globex or night market opens at 3:30 PM.

Figure 6.1 depicts the Face Peel trade and how it worked on April 1, 2008.

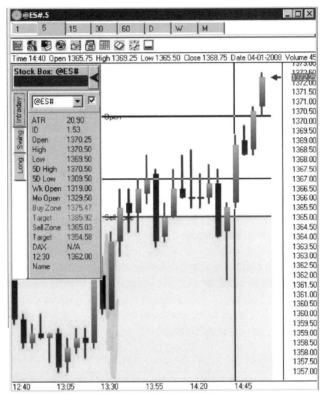

FIGURE 6.1 The Face Peel in action on April 1, 2008. The chart is a five-minute mini S&P chart generated on DTI's StockBox™ software.

Throughout this day the trend was up. At 2:30 PM the S&P was trading near 1363. Briefly, the bears attempted to shift market direction, but their efforts were weak. They were never able to cross the 2:30 PM price to the downside. When the attempt failed, the bulls took charge again and kept taking prices up until the close at 3:15 PM. The Face Peel was a nice end-of-the-day trade.

Figure 6.2 is a 30-minute chart that captures the daily move upward and the attempt of the bears to change the direction of the action.

Another great example of this trade in action was seen on March 18, 2008. On that date prices headed up all morning. The rally was a nice one. It was Fed Day, and at 1:15 PM, the Fed announced a 0.75-basis-point rate cut. The financial markets had already taken the rate reduction into consideration in pricing. Therefore, the markets initially reacted by taking prices down when the news was aired. However, around 2:00 PM, the bulls

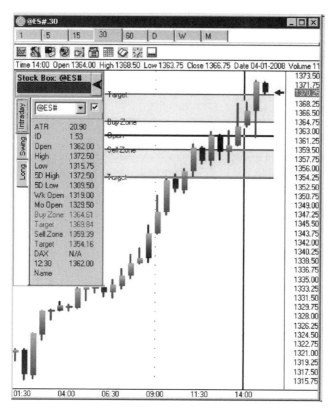

FIGURE 6.2 A 30-minute chart of the Face Peel on April 1, 2008.

decided to take control and push prices up again. At 2:30 PM, the mini S&P was trading at 1320. The bears briefly tried to gain the upper hand but were unable to break prices down below that 2:30 PM level. Therefore, a long play squeezed out the bears and paid the bulls handsomely. Those who stayed on the short side of things did, indeed, have their faces peeled. The session closed with a high of 1333.50. A full 13.5 points were made on the move as the session neared its close. At $50 per point, that makes a tidy sum to take to the bank. Figure 6.3 shows prices as the market neared its close. The prices are those recorded by the RoadMap™ software on that date. The E-mini S&P prices are recorded in the column on the far right under the symbol ESH8. At 2:15 (14:15 hours) the S&P was trading at 1319. The last price captured on the chart is 1329.50. However, the S&P actually closed slightly higher, at 1333.50. As the proprietary software used by DTI students shows, the S&P futures moved up sharply as the session came to a close.

	@ESH8	@YMH8	@NQH8	XGH8	EXH8	@ERH8	JINT.Z	TRIN.Z	@QMH8
14:00	1302.00	12154	1722.25	6359.50	3545.00	662.80	2084	0.58	99.975
14:15	1319.00	12285	1743.75	6425.50	3583.00	675.40	2427	0.45	99.975
14:30	1320.00	12297	1746.25	6426.50	3584.00	679.10	2462	0.46	99.975
Mini Pivot	1326.00	12345	1756.75	6457.00	3602.00	682.60	2502	0.41	99.975
ETR->	1329.50	12372	1760.50	6471.00	3610.00	682.10	2515	0.43	99.975

14:59:51 Tuesday, 03-18-2008

FIGURE 6.3 Prices from the RoadMap™ software on March 18, 2008.

Figure 6.4 is another look at the action. This is a 15-minute chart. After 2:30 PM, the direction was clearly up, up, and away. The bulls dominated the action for most of the day and did not cede any territory as the exchange moved into its closing final minutes.

The Face Peel was also profitable on March 27, 2008. Unlike the March 18, 2008, session, on this date the bears were leading the way throughout much of the day. The New York Stock Exchange (NYSE) issues and Nasdaq issues were running significantly negative during much of the session. At 2:30 PM, the bulls made an attempt to pull prices upward as the

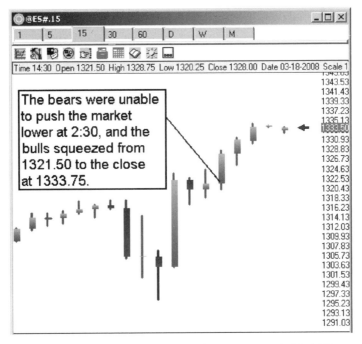

FIGURE 6.4 A 15-minute chart of the S&P futures on March 18, 2008.

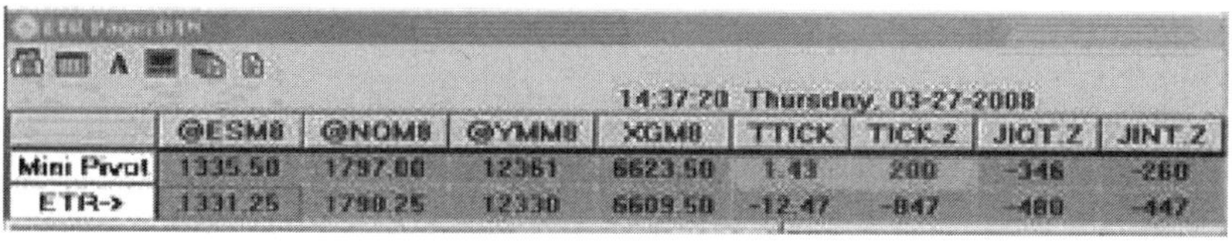

14:37:20 Thursday, 03-27-2008

	@ESM8	@NQM8	@YMM8	XGM8	TTICK	TICK.Z	JIQT.Z	JINT.Z
Mini Pivot	1335.50	1797.00	12361	6623.50	1.43	200	-346	-260
ETR->	1331.25	1790.25	12330	6609.50	-12.47	-847	-480	-447

FIGURE 6.5 On March 27, 2008, the RoadMap was red most of the day reflecting the negative sentiment of the market. At 2:37 PM, the TTICK was registering a negative 12.47, the NYSE tick was negative 847, and the issues on both the NYSE and the Nasdaq were very negative.

close neared. But, after a few minutes, it was clear that their efforts would not succeed. Below are charts of both the Nasdaq and the Dow. Figure 6.5 captures prices for both the Nasdaq and the Dow during the relevant time. The Nasdaq price is noted under the symbol NQM8 in column two and the Dow price appears under the symbol YMM8 in the third column. A trade on either of these indexes resulted in a respectable profit. As indicated in Figure 6.5, at 2:37 PM the Nasdaq was trading at 1790.25 and the Dow at 12330. All indicators were negative and pointing to a sell. When the bulls failed, the bears grew stronger. The bears are clearly in control.

The Custom Page on the RoadMap™ software tracks the action and records real-time data. When we were making the trade, the issues were extremely negative. Those prices are circled in Figure 6.6.

As time for the session's close neared, the mini Nasdaq fell about seven points in a few minutes. There was plenty of time to exit at the daily low and pick up $20 per point or $140 per contract. Those traders who were trading multiple contracts were able to pocket a little extra cash at the end of the day. In the final few minutes of the session there was some move up in prices, but traders had plenty of time to exit this trade with profits. Figure 6.7 charts the Nasdaq move.

On that same date, the Dow saw a much greater move downward. At 2:37 PM, the Dow was trading at 12330, and by 3:00 PM. It fell to a low of 12285. It was possible to make as much as 40 points on that trade. At $5 per point, that is about $200 per contract. It is true that prices tried to move up after hitting their lows. That is where the art of trading plays a major role. By using key numbers, I knew that support would probably enter the market at 12300. If the bulls succeeded in breaking through that price, I knew that the next area of support would be 12289. I knew this because historically both of these numbers are key numbers on the Dow. Knowing key numbers allows traders to maximize profits and avoid risk. Those who held the trade to the close on this day did not make money because once the 12289 price held, the bulls pulled prices back up. But good tape reading and risk management skills should have made traders aware of the danger of holding positions once the 12289 price held. Trading is an art and not a

Symbol	Open	Last
@ESM8	1335.00	1331.25
@YMM8	12378	12330
@NQM8	1807.75	1790.25
XGM8	6540.00	6603.50
TTICK	3.48	-12.47
TICK.Z	5	-847
JINT.Z	543	-447
JIQT.Z	457	-480
OIH	176.96	175.76
QID	48.36	49.54
DUG	38.18	38.44
V	64.05	63.91
@QMK8	106.20	107.175
AAPL	144.95	140.49
@USM8	119.025	118.05
BIDU	237.000	237.4100
EXM8	3517.00	3548.00
BSC	11.40	11.02
@ERM8	637.40	634.80
@DXM8	71.90	72.31
CFC	6.17	5.85

FIGURE 6.6 The Custom Page from the RoadMap™ software captures the price data at 2:37 PM on March 27, 2008. The NYSE issues (JINT.Z) are negative 447. The Nasdaq issues (JIQT.Z) are negative 480.

science. It involves gauging a number of factors and making wise decisions based on market data. Figure 6.8 charts the action on the mini Dow futures on March 27, 2008.

For many years the hours of operation for the mini Dow futures were slightly different than the hours for the mini S&P 500 futures and the mini Nasdaq futures. However, the Dow is now part of the CME Group, and the trading hours are identical to those for other equity index futures traded

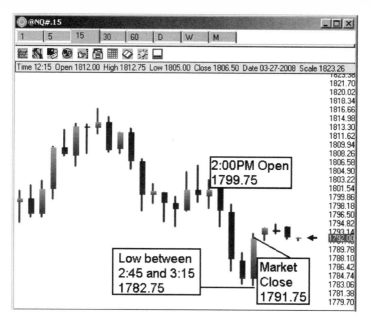

FIGURE 6.7 A 15-minute chart of the Nasdaq futures on March 27, 2008. A sell offered a nice end-of-the-day paycheck.

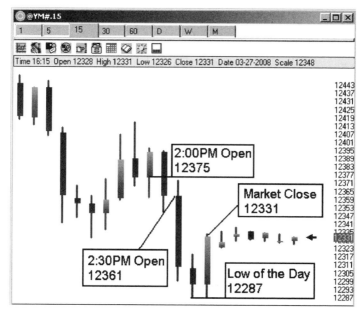

FIGURE 6.8 The general trend of prices throughout the day was down. After 2:30 PM the bulls tried to change the situation, but initially failed. Prices dropped as low as the low 12290s. After hitting those lows, the bulls finally did make some hay and pulled prices up a few points at the close. Nevertheless, those with good tape-reading skills had plenty of time to take some cash home.

at the CME. I always look for opportunities to make the Face Peel trade because it tends to be a good one for my students and me.

OFF TO THE RACES

Another futures breakout trade that I enjoy is a Nasdaq trade that I call "Off to the Races." Again this is a futures trade, and it is definitely a day trade. The Nasdaq futures are a derivative of the Nasdaq 100 index. They are also traded at the CME, and the hours of operation are the same as those for the S&P futures. There are several Nasdaq contracts. A big contract trades for $100 per point and a mini contract for $20 per point. Margin requirements are similar to those for the S&P. Therefore, there is good leverage to allow traders to maximize trading dollars.

This trade is executed in the morning one hour after the exchange opens. I look to make this trade under the following conditions: the NYSE issues and the Nasdaq issues (these indicators are explained in Chapter 4) must be either greater than or less than 500 and the overall market must be trending either up or down. In other words, this is a trending trade. The criteria seem simple, but the trade, when it sets up, can be a good one.

I made this trade on March 26, 2008. On that date, oil news had been released. Every Wednesday morning the Energy Information Administration reports the oil inventory numbers. March 26, 2008, was one of those reporting days. The Nasdaq (NQM8) was trading at 1810.75. The NYSE issues were extremely negative at −1062 (JINT.Z) and the Nasdaq issues were almost as bad at −904 (JIQT.Z). With the issues reading so strongly negative, I would not suggest taking a long position. I went short at 1811 on the Nasdaq. I was targeting an ultimate profit of 15 points. However, to reduce risk and insure some green. I bought back some of my contracts with a six- or seven-point gain. My initial stop/loss was 20 points above my entry price. That represents 20 percent of the average true range (ATR), and I never like to risk much more than that amount on any trade. After liquidating one-third of my contracts for six or seven points of profit, I moved my stop/loss order down 10 points. Now my risk was only 10 points on each remaining contract. As prices continued to move in my favor, I trailed the market and insured that this trade would be a moneymaker for me. Figure 6.9 shows the prices that were recorded on the RoadMap™ software just after 9:30.

THE FAST DANCE

The "Fast Dance" is a Dow trade that I enter and exit very quickly. The Dow is traded at the Chicago Board of Trade (CBOT). In 2007, the CBOT merged

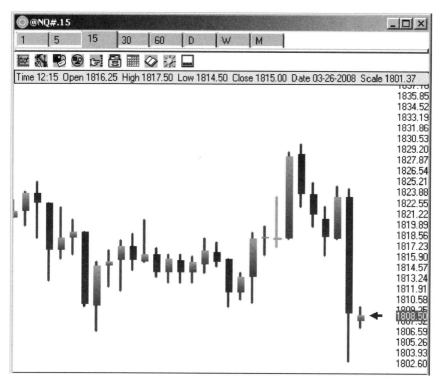

FIGURE 6.9 A 15-minute Nasdaq chart on March 26, 2008. The Nasdaq trade was made as prices moved down in the long bar that is the second one from the far right.

with the CME and became part of its financial holdings. Like other equity index futures, there are two Dow contracts. The big Dow trades for $10 per point and the mini trades for $5. That feature of the mini Dow makes it a great place for beginning futures traders to learn the ropes. The hours of the mini Dow are identical to those for the mini Nasdaq and the mini S&P. Electronic trading begins at 3:30 PM on Monday through Thursday. On Sunday, trading starts at 5:00 PM. The electronic exchange closes the following day at 3:15 PM. Again, margin requirements are similar to those for the other index futures. Also, if one holds contracts from session to session, he is holding positions overnight and a far greater margin or account balance is required. For that reason, I prefer day trading these futures contracts.

When I trade the Dow, I go long on the ones and short on the nines. Many Dow traders may disagree with this approach but through observation I have determined that for my strategies these entry points are most advantageous.

The "Fast Dance" is an afternoon trade. When traders return from lunch, they tend to evaluate the morning action and either reverse it or accelerate it. Therefore, this trade is based on trading just after 1:00 PM. I use my software, the RoadMap™ and StockBox™, to gauge the sentiment of the market, but it is possible to execute the trade without these aids. It is just a little harder to do so.

First, evaluate the major futures indexes. Look at the S&P, the Nasdaq, the Dax, and the Dow. Are they all moving in the same direction? If so, how pronounced is that movement? In other words, is there an ascertainable bullish or bearish sentiment expressed in the futures indexes? Measure this mood by looking at the 12:30 PM prices and compare those prices to the 1:00 PM prices. Are prices higher or lower at 1:00 PM than at 12:30? If they are higher, I look to buy the mini Dow futures or the S&P futures. If they are lower, I will sell. As the trade name indicates, this is a fast trade and I get into and out of it quickly. In fact, I may be in this trade for only a few minutes. "Grim Reaper," a very volatile and unpredictable time in the financial markets, begins at 1:30 PM, and I generally want to be out of the position and on the sidelines by that time. If I am in a trade and making money, I may stay with it and watch prices carefully, but I will not add new positions.

In the S&P Fast Dance on April 25, 2008, the high of the range between 12:30 PM and 1:00 PM was 1390.75. I bought some positions at 1391.75 with a 3.5 point profit target. With this trade on the S&P, we use a 3.5 point initial stop. On this date the initial target was reached and surpassed. It was possible to make 10 points on the trade. However, because the trade continued to pay, it was not until 2:00 PM that the full potential of the move was realized. Figure 6.10 tells the story.

On this date the dance was a waltz rather than a jitterbug. Figure 6.10 is a 30-minute chart of the E-mini on April 25, 2008. The lower horizontal arrow shows our entry point and the slanting upward arrow highlights the nice move up. This was a trade that paid.

THE SQUEAKY WHEEL

In addition to trading equity index futures, I also trade other futures contracts like gold and crude oil. Like the trades above, the "Squeaky Wheel" is a breakout trade, a day trade, and a futures trade. Crude oil is traded at the New York Mercantile Exchange (NYMEX). Other products traded at this exchange include a variety of fuels like gasoline, electricity, heating oil, and coal. Metals are also traded here including gold, silver, and copper. Those who want to buy a bulk of crude can do so and delivery of

FIGURE 6.10 The 30-minute S&P 500 E-mini futures chart shows the "Fast Dance" on April 25, 2008. The small horizontal arrow points to the entry point for the trade. Once prices broke above the price bar that was formed beween 12:30 and 1:00 PM central time, prices moved up.

1000 barrels of oil per contract will be delivered to Cushing, Oklahoma, for pickup.

As for me, I am looking for a cheap way to fuel my auto but I am not in the market for 1000 barrels of crude. Therefore, I trade the futures and try to make the cash to pay those high prices at the pump. Options are also traded at the NYMEX. There is a big oil contract and a mini contract. The mini contract is valued at $500 per point and there are 40 ticks per point, giving each tick a value of 12.5 cents. The big contract is worth $1000 per point. There are 100 ticks per point and each tick is worth $10. The open outcry pits of the NYMEX open at 9:00 AM and close at 2:30 PM. Like the S&P and Nasdaq contracts, crude futures trade on the Globex after hours. Globex trading begins at 6:00 PM and closes at 5:15 PM the following day.

As with other futures contracts a margin account is required. The money deposited into the trading account is a "good-faith" deposit or performance bond. The amount of funds required is established by the exchange based on their risk assessment. The web site for the NYMEX explains the danger of trading with margin with an example of gold futures. Per the exchange, you can trade a gold futures contract for a "good-faith" deposit between $2500 and $3375 per contract. However, the value of the gold controlled by that contract is around $90,000. To me, that means that there can be big risk and big reward associated with this product.

Each day after trading comes to a close, the exchange marks-to-market the contract. The exchange determines whether the day's trading has resulted in a gain or loss. If there is a loss such that additional funds are needed, a margin call will be issued.

I make the "Squeaky Wheel" trade on Wednesdays. I do so because each Wednesday at 9:30 AM central time the Energy Information Administration (EIA), a statistical arm of the Department of Energy, releases its weekly petroleum status report. A few years back I never paid any attention to this weekly bit of news. However, with the onset of the war in Iraq, tribal fighting in Nigeria, industrialization in China, and other major world factors including the dropping price of the dollar on the world market, fuel supplies are sometimes stressed and prices go wild. Therefore, I always listen intently to the weekly status report. The EIA monitors our nation's petroleum inventories. These inventories consist of both domestic and foreign products.

PEARL 8

Every Wednesday a crude oil report is released at 9:30 AM. There are premarket trading opportunities in the crude sector the morning of the announcement. Go to www.dtitrader.com to view this trade in action.

Following the report, I generally trade. Because I often trade crude oil, I chart prices. I track the yearly opening price, the monthly opens, and each weekly open. In that way, it is easy to see in a glance the direction the market is moving. At the time of this writing, there has been no question as to direction—prices have been going up.

I note the price just before the news airs. I look for a 0.50-point movement. I trade in that direction. As a rule, this tends to be a fast-paced trade that is over quickly. Only traders who have the ability to execute trades rapidly should attempt this trade. The symbol for mini light sweet crude is QM. Many of my students made this trade on May 1, 2008. Figure 6.11 depicts the fall of crude when news was reported.

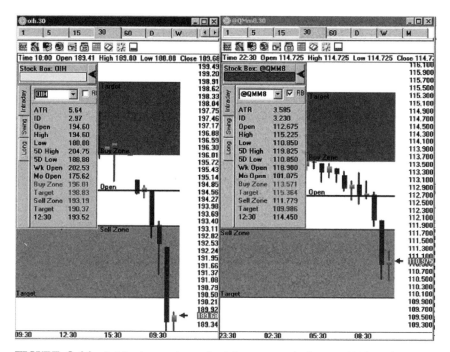

FIGURE 6.11 A 30-minute chart of mini sweet crude futures (QM) and OIH on May 1, 2008, following a news release about oil inventories. The bar chart on the left is OIH, which is an oil exchange-traded fund. The sweet crude oil chart is on the right. A short play with either OIH or crude futures made a nice play.

PEARL 9

Crude oil tends to have a negative close on the last trading day of the month.

REVIEW

I am a professional trader and I have been trading for many years. Consequently, I trade a variety of products and employ various strategies to make money. One of the strategies that I use is a breakout move. I look for prices to break above or below an established level and I go with the trend. I use this breakout move to trade a variety of futures products. I make the "Face Peel" trade on the S&P E-mini futures. This trade is made in the afternoon as trading at the CME nears an end for the session. It takes advantage of a big market move that has occurred during the session. The trader lucky enough to catch this play is able to ride the trend to the close and get some fast cash.

I also do a Nasdaq trade that I call "Off to the Races." I use the NYSE issues and the Nasdaq issues to make this trade. It is made around 9:00 AM, and it is made only if both of the noted issues are greater than 500 plus or minus. The trade is made as prices break out from the 9:00 AM price in agreement with the sentiment of the market.

A third breakout trade that I make is the "Fast Dance." This is an afternoon trade and is executed after the lunch break. When traders return to the markets after enjoying a short hiatus, they often reaffirm their morning positions by adding to them or they shift gears and change positions. For that reason, this trade can be a winner. It is a Dow futures trade based on the price range between 12:30 and 1:00 PM. With indicator and market support, if prices break above or below that 30-minute range, I join the move and buy or sell as indicated. This is a quick trade, and I generally liquidate my positions by 1:30 PM. I do not want to be in a risky position when the "Grim Reaper" is looking for victims.

In addition to equity index futures, I also use the breakout move to trade commodities. Every Wednesday I anticipate an oil crude futures trade based on the weekly oil status reports. These reports are made public at 9:30 AM and with crude under stress, prices respond to the news. I identify the sentiment of traders and get on the winning team. One of my favorite vehicles for trading oil news is OIH, an oil-based exchange-traded fund.

Always remember to respect risk and be an informed and knowledgeable trader. The strategies detailed in this chapter involve trading futures contracts. That means that a futures account is required and risk of loss is great—especially for those who are uneducated and inexperienced. Learn about these risks and understand them before trading futures contracts.

CHAPTER 7

News Pays

T raders—especially day traders—live for big news events. News moves markets. Home sales are lower than expected and the markets sell off. The Consumer Price Index data indicates that inflation is threatening the economy. Traders fear that the Fed will raise interest rates to keep prices under control. Stock prices tank. Likewise, if good news is reported, the markets salute the numbers and go up. Therefore, traders need to understand how to use news to make money. News is so important to the markets that I plan my trading week around the major reports that will be released. I want to be informed and ready when the numbers are known so that I can maximize the moneymaking opportunity that is presented.

Many governmental and institutional economic reports are published each month. These reports cover all aspects of our economy. Some studies gauge manufacturing output; some count new home sales, housing starts, or existing home sales; while others track consumer habits like spending or confidence. Many of these reports are released at the same time each month. That is, some may be released on the first Friday of the month or the third Thursday, and so on. Therefore, a trader has the opportunity to know when important news is being broadcast, and he or she can be prepared to trade it. The first step to using any news strategy is learning the day and time when the information will be made public. The easy way to do this is to keep a calendar and use the calendar to benefit from the news. Following are some of the market-moving news reports to watch and possibly trade.

Consumer confidence is one of the important gauges of perceived market health. There are two reports that traders watch: the *Conference Board*

Consumer Confidence Index and the University of Michigan's *Consumer Sentiment Index*. The Consumer Confidence Index is a compilation of data derived from a survey of consumer attitudes about the health of the economy. This survey is conducted by a business-backed research group based in New York. Each month, this group surveys 5000 consumers across the United States. This data reflects patterns in consumer attitudes and spending. When consumers believe that the economy is not doing well, they tend to tighten their belts and spend less. Likewise, if they believe that the economy and their personal financial health is in good condition, they are more likely to spend freely. Obviously, consumers who are optimistic about the future will be more willing to buy items that they need and want. Because consumer spending accounts for more than two-thirds of the overall economy, the financial markets respond to consumer confidence data.

Another report that reflects consumer confidence is the University of Michigan study. This report was first compiled in the 1940s, and it is respected and watched by many traders. Like the Consumer Confidence Index, this data reflects attitudes of consumers and their pessimism or optimism about the overall health of the economy. The financial markets often react irrationally. That is, emotion may be the driving force behind a rally or a sell-off. For that reason, the attitude of consumers about the economy is very significant, making these regularly scheduled economic reports important to the markets and to traders.

The *Consumer Price Index (CPI)* is a measure of the average price level of a fixed basket of goods and services purchased by consumers each month. The items in the basket and the services purchased remain constant month after month so that price changes may be tracked and inflation monitored. This report is the most widely followed indicator of inflation in the United States. When inflation is up, consumers spend more money for their living expenses and cash is siphoned from the economy. Interest rates also rise as the Federal Reserve's Open Market Committee works to slow inflation and keep the economy moving at an optimum rate. The CPI has the power to be a real market mover. It is watched closely by governmental entities and traders.

This is one economic report you do not want to miss. Traders around the world listen intently to the CPI numbers because they know the repercussions of rising inflation. This is an important report for the general economy and for the financial markets.

Durable goods orders reflect the new orders placed with domestic manufacturers for immediate and future delivery of factory hard goods like automobiles, appliances, and computers. This data is compiled by the Department of Commerce and reflects both consumer demand and business spending. There are advance reports and follow-up reports. Often, there are revised reports as well. These statistics are also carefully watched by the financial markets. If the economy is growing too quickly, inflation may result. If factory orders are dropping, recession may be in the cards. Durable goods orders tell investors what they can expect from the manufacturing sector. If fewer durable goods are being ordered, factories will slow down production, which will likely cause a further shrinking of the overall economy. This report is released at 7:30 AM near the end of each month. The stock market often responds to this data.

Existing home sales data is gathered by the National Association of Realtors and reflects the number of previously constructed homes in which a sale closed during the month. This group also tracks data about the average prices of homes. Existing homes account for a larger share of the housing market than new homes and indicate housing market trends. At the time of this writing, the housing and mortgage sectors are under stress and investors are keeping a close eye on both of them.

Housing sales, both existing home sales and new house sales, have a big effect on the overall economy because house purchases have a huge rippling effect. When houses are bought, a mortgage is generally secured so the banking and financial sector is affected. Then there is furniture, appliances, and other products to buy in order to fix up and furnish the house. A healthy housing market bodes well for the overall economy. Conversely, a weak one scares the markets and is evidence that the economy is ailing. Furniture, appliances, and other consumer goods may sit on showroom floors instead of making their way out of the door of manufacturers and distributors and into homes across America.

Gross domestic product (GDP) is the broadest measure of aggregate economic activity. This is a government-generated report, and it is one of the best indicators of the overall health of the economy because it encompasses consumer spending, business and residential investment, and price indexes. If there is growth or shrinkage in the U.S. economy, this report will capture the data. This report is released at 7:30 AM.

Like the CPI, the GDP has the power to be a big market mover. Mark this one on the economic calendar and be ready to watch the markets and see how they respond to it. This data is important for government, business, consumers, and traders.

Housing starts measure the initial construction of residential units each month. This report is important for a number of reasons, including the demand for building products, construction labor, appliances, furniture, and the like. Housing construction has a major ripple effect on the economy. That makes this report important for traders and investors.

New home sales measures the number of newly constructed homes that have sold during the month. The level of new home sales indicates housing market trends. Like housing starts, this data may also result in a ripple effect in the economy because those new home buyers need furniture, appliances, and other household items. This data reflects the optimism or pessimism of consumers. If times are good and consumers are confident in the future, they will be more likely to purchase a home. The flip side is that if they fear that the economy is slowing down or that bad times are ahead, they will postpone such a large purchase as a home. Therefore, this report tells us a great deal about the confidence level of consumers. When news on the housing front is especially good or especially bad, the financial markets will likely react. That makes housing news a potential market mover to watch.

The *Producer Price Index (PPI)* is released monthly by the U.S. Department of Labor. This report measures price changes for products that are produced. It measures the average changes of selling prices over time. Because the U.S. economy is large and diversified, there are many PPIs generated each month. In fact, the Department of Labor compiles over 10,000 of them. The data gathered is then analyzed and merged into one report.

Like the CPI, the PPI tracks the same data each month. Because this report reflects cost and price data from producers, it foreshadows prices for consumers and the general economy. Inflationary signals may be revealed before they hit the retail level. For this reason, the PPI is important to governmental and business decision makers.

Since the PPI measures prices of consumer goods and capital equipment, a portion of the inflation at the producer level will also be reflected in the CPI. By tracking price pressures in the pipeline, investors can anticipate inflationary consequences in coming months. The PPI is considered a precursor of both consumer price inflation and producer profits. If the prices paid to manufacturers increase, businesses are faced with either charging higher prices or cutting profits. Both the CPI and the PPI are important inflation gauges and are deemed to be significant to traders and investors. Again, this report is released at 7:30 AM.

Retail sales measure the total receipts at stores that sell durable and nondurable goods. Consumer spending accounts for two-thirds of the GDP and is therefore a key element in economic growth. This data has a great influence on the financial markets, especially during key times like the Christmas holiday season. Retail sales are very telling in that the data says a great deal about the confidence of consumers and the numbers may also be a good predictor about future economic activity. If sales are low, production will slow down and both retail and manufacturing layoffs may result. This data has the power to be a big market mover.

Barron's is a great source for economic and market information. I regularly check the *Barron's* economic calendar and make notes of important events to watch. In addition, some of the information about the preceding financial and economic reports was derived from *Barron's* and their online site. For more information about regularly scheduled economic reports and the exact times that reports are released, you may want to visit www.barrons.com or the site of my trading educational facility at www.dtitrader.com. We also keep an economic calendar for our students so that they can be ready for news.

Obviously, if you are going to trade news and use these market-moving events effectively, it is imperative that you know the dates and times when the reports and data will be released. Keep your own economic calendar and use it to schedule your trading time.

PEARL 10

Know when important economic data is being reported. Then use that information to make money.

NEVER PREDICT THE MARKET

Losers predict—winners react. More than one trader has lost his shirt by trying to guess the market's response to news. I never try to predict the news, and I never attempt to anticipate the market's response to news. Experience has taught me the dangers of such a policy. Any experienced trader knows that there are times when seemingly good news is aired, but the markets expected better so there is a sell-off. Or bad news breaks and investors were prepared for the situation to be even worse, so in the aftermath of the bad data, the markets rally. Having observed this phenomenon hundreds of time, I have learned to wait for the numbers and the market's reaction; let the market lead the way, and follow.

Once the numbers in a particular report are known, there is generally a rapid and very pronounced response. Prices may surge up or down in seconds. Then, after a couple of minutes have passed, traders have digested the information and may have a more measured and calmer reaction. For that reason, beginners should never trade news. It is too easy to get on the wrong side of an immediate and irrational response and lose money. News spikes are generally very brief. I always advise beginners to wait a couple of minutes after the news has aired, then assess the market and make a move.

STRATEGIES FOR EARLY NEWS

In the United States, 7:30 AM is a prime time for the release of a variety of economic reports. The CPI, PPI, GDP, retail sales, and housing starts are only a few of the major reports that are published at this time. To maximize trading, consider the time of day and the information and indicators available at this time. First, you will recall that 7:30 AM news falls within Time Segment 2; Asian exchanges have closed and the day's trading session in the United States has not yet begun. But in Paris, London, Frankfurt, and across Europe, financial markets are active. I use the Dax futures as an indicator of sentiment. The 6:00 AM Dax price is a benchmark for me. Before the news is released, I write down that important 6:00 AM number. Then I am able to gauge the market in relation to its movement above or below that price. I also look at the other futures indexes like the S&P, Dow, and Nasdaq. In relation to the Globex or nightly highs and lows, where are these indexes trading just before the news is known? Are they near their lows or their highs? If the futures indexes are trading near the nightly lows, that is probably an indication that traders are anticipating some bad news. Likewise, if they are trading near their nightly highs, traders are likely expecting good report data. If, in fact, the news is good, prices should surge upward and there should be new Globex highs as a result of the information. Or, if the news is negative, there should quickly be new lows.

If the market fails to make a new low on "bad" news or a new high on "good" news, take note. Here is how I use that information. If "bad" news is not bad enough to pull prices down to a new low, prices are likely going up. Therefore, I see it as an early buying chance. The reverse is also true. If the "good" news is not good enough to merit a major play by the bulls, I sell. As confirmation that my analysis is correct, I check the E-mini and the Dax. The Dax is probably moving up in price while the E-mini S&P is trying to test the lows. When the S&P cannot break through those lows, it changes direction and I make money.

Figure 7.1 is a chart of the E-mini S&P futures that depicts this trade. On May 17, 2007, the Globex high on the E-mini was 1518. News was released and prices tried to move up above the high but could not do so. Figure 7.1 shows the market's response when the bulls were unable to move above the highs. A market that cannot go up generally goes down, and that is what happened on May 17, 2007.

Another strategy for trading the 7:30 AM news is to gauge prices before the news breaks as outlined above. That is, look at the Dax 6:00 AM price and use it as a benchmark. Also note prices in the S&P, Nasdaq, and Dow to determine if those indexes are trading near their highs or lows. If the bulls or the bears are able to reach a new high or a new low, wait for prices to settle and retrace. It is highly likely that after a few minutes they will do so. If there is a strong sentiment in a particular direction, the move will be repeated and you will have a chance to buy or sell on the confirmation move. So, buy or sell on the second pass above the new low or new high.

As the chart in Figure 7.2 shows, this was a good play on May 11, 2007. The second upward pass on the E-mini S&P was a great play for day traders.

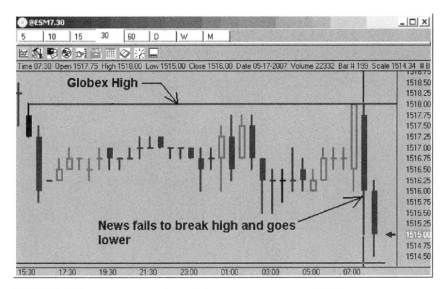

FIGURE 7.1 A 30-minute chart of the E-mini on May 17, 2007.

At DTI, we regularly trade news. On May 2, 2008, employment news was released. The employment situation data was predicted to be bleak. However, when the news was reported, the numbers were far better than analysts had hoped. Anytime there is a significant deviation from the predicted numbers, the market reacts. On this day there was a big move up and

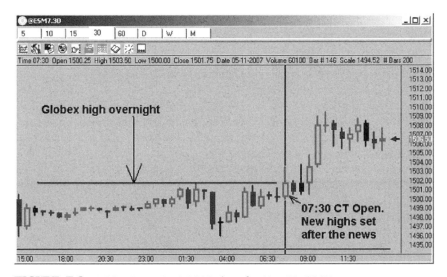

FIGURE 7.2 A 30-minute E-mini S&P chart for May 11, 2007.

FIGURE 7.3 A 30-minute chart of the E-mini S&P 500 futures shows the news break. Because this is an after-hours time frame, the data recorded begins on May 1, 2008. The trade was made on May 2, 2008, with the 7:30 AM central time news release. Prices shot up on the news and then settled down after digesting it. With my new software, NewsTrader™, I was able to use the news to make money.

we were able to take some profits from the market. We traded the E-mini S&P futures, and the trade is charted in Figure 7.3.

Again, those who are beginners should never try to trade a news event because prices are too unpredictable. As the above chart shows, after traders considered the move, prices gradually moved down. A trader has to be quick and right to make money at the time the news comes out. That takes experience and practice. Practice and hone your skills with a simulation; not when money is on the line.

A 9:00 NEWS STRATEGY

The first thing to note about this strategy is the time that it is employed. At 9:00 AM we are trading in Time Segment 3. The day-trading session in the United States has begun. American financial markets are leading the way and the world is looking to our shores. Also note that at this time, the open outcry pits at the Chicago Mercantile Exchange (CME) have been operating for 30 minutes. I use the high and the low of this time frame as a benchmark to gauge sentiment and evaluate prices. For example, say the high of the S&P during this time is 1348 and the low is 1340; if prices break above the high of the 30-minute range (1348), I consider the move bullish, and below it (1340) I deem it bearish.

I use all of the data available to me. That is, before making this trade, I look at the Dax to determine whether it is above or below its 6:00 AM price. I look at the other futures indexes to get a sense of the market's mood. Are they making new highs, new lows, or just hanging out? I also check indicators like the NYSE issues and the Nasdaq issues, and other statistical data. However, I have one other important bit of data that can help me at this particular time – I look at that 8:30 to 9:00 AM price bar on the S&P E-mini futures. If prices move above that bar with support from the indexes and indicators, I join the bulls and buy. If they move down with that same support, I sell.

Although it is a few minutes later, I also trade news at 9:30 AM, especially on Wednesday. On Wednesday, the EIA releases its weekly report on petroleum inventories. A few years ago, I had never even heard of this particular bit of news. However, with oil prices rising and supplies threatened, this regularly scheduled news event is closely watched by millions of traders around the world. On April 30, 2008, I tuned into the news and made money. On that date, oil inventories were anticipated to be up by 900,000 barrels of crude. However, when the news broke, the actual figure was 3.8 million barrels. In other words, inventories were significantly higher than expected. Since supplies were up, crude prices immediately fell. I shorted an oil constructed exchange-traded fund (ETF)—OIH. OIH is traded on the American Exchange. I went short at 197.66. Within five minutes, the shares had dropped two dollars and within two hours they fell about another two. However, when I made the trade, I exited some of my positions quickly with a small profit. My game plan is to make some fast money to cover any potential losses. Then I can hold a smaller portion of my positions without risking my personal money. I have taken some of the market's cash, and I am funding my trade with the market's money.

Figure 7.4 shows the OIH trade on April 30, 2008. The chart was generated on my StockBox™ software and contains a good bit of information. However, the important aspect of the chart to note is how prices fell in response to the news. The chart on the far left is a five-minute OIH chart. The chart on the right is a crude oil futures chart. Both crude futures and OIH fell quickly in response to the good news about supplies of crude.

The preceding trade was made with a new piece of software that has been developed by DTI. The software is known as the NewsTrader™. Prior

FIGURE 7.4 The chart on the far right is a chart of OIH. The chart on the left is a chart of sweet crude oil futures. These charts were generated on my StockBox™ software. The data in the darkened boxes contains information DTI students need, like the monthly and weekly opens and the daily highs and lows. The trade of OIH or sweet crude was a nice one.

to a news event, users of the software research the event and determine the market's forecast for that particular bit of news. A site that gives the forecast is www.forexfactory.com. By going to this site, it is possible to learn what traders and experts around the world think the numbers will be. For example, if the GDP numbers are being reported, NewsTrader™ users need to know what the market expects the numbers to look like. Then they are able to place orders to take advantage of unexpected numbers that might be reported or deviations from the anticipated data that might result in a profitable market move. The idea is that the market will react strongly to unexpected news if that news is significant enough. Consider again the GDP. If bad numbers are predicted but the economy does better than anticipated, the good statistics will shock the market and there will likely be a rally. Once the NewsTrader™ is properly programmed, it makes the trade for the user.

Because the markets react so quickly to news, it is difficult to trade the news without having the ability to receive news releases and data quickly. Therefore, the NewsTrader™ is tied into a news service. The program receives the information and in milliseconds the trade is executed.

The NewsTrader™ software is a great example of how I change and adapt to market conditions. A short time ago, I did not attempt to trade the news the second it was released. Without the right equipment, such a strategy is too dangerous. However, by designing the NewsTrader™ and having a subscription to a news service, my students and I are able to use a new strategy and make money in a slightly different way. Successful traders must be as dynamic as the markets they trade.

EARNINGS SEASON AND HOW TO USE IT

Four times during the year, traders get another news bonus—earnings season. At a specified time during the month, corporations tell the public how they are doing. The big guys usually do not reveal their numbers until the NYSE closes. But those who trade after hours still have a chance to trade the news. Here is what I do to prepare for earnings reports.

First, I visit www.earnings.com and check to see which corporations will be reporting. If you do not know when the earnings data is released, you cannot trade it. I am only interested in large corporations. By that I mean those that are the largest on the S&P 500, the Nasdaq 100, or the Dow 30. Once I find some really big fish that I might want to catch, I do a little research and determine how the public generally responds to earnings information for these companies. I look at the last few quarters. When earnings data was released, what happened to the stock price? Did it go up or down? Was the move large or moderate? I want a stock that generally has big market moves when earnings are announced. The move can be up or down, the direction is irrelevant. What matters is that this stock is so important to the market that the price moves when the data is released. Finally, I check to see if the company has been meeting expectations or not.

After I identify the stocks that I want to trade, I generally wait for the announcement before trading. Like other news events, I do not guess about earnings. However, occasionally, if I have what I believe to be very strong analysis on which to judge a probable play, I may trade options for that particular stock. One such trade was made in the first quarter of 2008 with Apple. The entire market was down and had been trading down for several weeks. By looking at the yearly open, the monthly open, and the weekly open, I decided that Apple would likely be a sell. However, I know that I do not have a crystal ball. Therefore, I did not short Apple ahead of the announcement. Instead, I bought puts. That allowed me to define and control my risk while also taking advantage of an Apple sell-off. Once earnings came out, the stock price quickly fell from the 155 area to 120. I was loving it! That was a great earnings trade for me. Figure 7.5 charts Apple's downward dive. For more information about trading options refer to Chapter 12.

FIGURE 7.5 Daily chart of Apple that spans most of the month of January 2008. When earnings were reported, Apple shares dropped.

Because earnings generally are announced after the stock market closes, other than options, I use the index futures to make most of my plays. This is how I do it. I follow the same strategies as noted earlier. That is, I identify big players on the S&P 500, the Nasdaq 100, and the Dow 30. Once their numbers come out, I trade the index after hours. If a big tech stock listed on the Nasdaq 100 reports worse-than-expected numbers, I can trade that news by shorting the Nasdaq in after-hours trading. Of course, in addition to trading on the basis of earnings, I also do my usual analysis for trading futures before executing a trade. If all of the indicators are against my move, I wait. I know I cannot fight the market. I want to correctly identify the direction of the current and move with it to profits.

CAUTION

Trading news can be tricky. Prices may jump and gyrate wildly on news. Therefore, as noted earlier, I never recommend that beginning traders trade news events. It is simply too risky to do so. Before trading news, you need to know the dangers involved. You also need to have the skills required to exit the trade quickly should such a move be necessary. For all of these reasons, only experienced traders who possess the requisite skills to swim in these shark-infested waters should attempt to trade the news.

PEARL 11

The night of the presidential election offers great trading opportunities after 7:00 PM central time.

BREAKING NEWS

In addition to regularly scheduled economic reports, other news alters the financial outlook and reverberates through Wall Street. Some breaking news events that can make or break a trade include a terrorist attack, a federal investigation of a major corporation, and a good or bad but unexpected news announcement from a blue-chip firm. These items and many more like them have the ability to move prices.

Due to the nature of life, it is impossible to predict or prepare for such events. Recent examples of market-moving breaking news include the unexpected Fed rate cut following the Martin Luther King holiday. The market rallied off the lows. Another example is the Bear Stearns Corporation and its near-bankruptcy scare. The news took the markets by surprise, and traders responded by selling off.

The best action you can take to protect your money from breaking news is to always use a protective stop when trading. That is, when an order is executed, put in an order to remove you from the market should the trade go significantly against your position. There are a number of strategies for selecting the exact place to put a stop/loss order, but I will not discuss them all here. The big idea is to identify the maximum loss that you are willing to take on the trade or the price point where you know you are wrong on the trade and put the stop/loss order there. Even in the face of unexpected news that moves prices against your trade, if the markets remain calm and orderly, you should be removed from the action with a small loss instead of a big one. Therefore, ALWAYS USE STOP/LOSS ORDERS. Nothing moves the financial markets like news. Learn to use news to make money.

PEARL 12

Markets respect news. You should, too.

REVIEW

Each month, an array of research and resulting economic reports are released by various institutions and governmental entities. Most of this information is publicized at either 7:30 or 9:00 AM central time. Traders who follow both the news and the markets can use this information to make money. The first step to trading news is scheduling; know when important news will be released and be prepared. When each month begins, check an economic calendar and plan accordingly.

If you wish to trade a news event, get ready in advance. Study prices and indicators before the news breaks. Identify the price points that will signal a buy or a sell and be prepared to act quickly. When it comes to news, the early bird gets the worm.

In addition to news reports like the CPI or existing home sales, corporations regularly release information. Earnings season also brings opportunities. Do your research and identify some stocks to trade. Then watch the numbers and make your play.

Only experienced traders should trade news, as prices can move quickly and those on the wrong side of a news play can lose a great deal of money in the blink of an eye. Unseasoned traders should sit on the sidelines and wait for the initial excitement of news to pass. Once the mania is over, it is easier to see the true direction of the market and trade it.

Finally, breaking news is also important to the markets. However, there is no way to anticipate it or prepare for it. Therefore, it is very important to always use a stop/loss order to get you out of a market that is strongly going against your position.

CHAPTER 8

Making Money with Bernanke

My heart is racing and my hands are damp. I have made this trade dozens of times, but my adrenaline still surges as I wait for the news. Today, I am in Dallas visiting Penson, a large brokerage firm. I, like the rest of the world, am waiting for Ben Bernanke to speak. I know the information he releases will give me an opportunity to make money. I do not plan to miss my chance—even though I am miles from home and the comforts and equipment of my office.

As I wait for the news, I look closely at prices and consider potential buy and sell points. It is Fed Day, and I always trade the regularly scheduled Fed rate announcement. Eight times a year, the Federal Open Market Committee (FOMC) meets and discusses the overall health of the U.S. economy. They look carefully at inflationary gauges and consider price trends in the context of the increasing or decreasing patterns of industrial and business operations. One of the most important jobs of the Federal Reserve is to regulate monetary policy in such a way that full employment is fostered while simultaneously holding inflation in check. A powerful tool available to the Fed is the federal funds rate. At each of these scheduled meetings, the Fed announces its decision about any rate changes. As a rule, when the news is released, the markets go wild. It is impossible to predict with any degree of certainty how Wall Street will respond to any particular rate announcement, but there will be a reaction.

Knowing my habit of trading the Fed, the executives at Penson offer me a desk and Internet access so that I can ply my trade. Not only am I making the trade myself, but I am doing so over the DTI chat room; and it is packed with observers. The area in which I am sitting is also filled with

99

spectators from Penson who are eyeing the market and waiting for me to trade it. The fact that my actions are being observed by so many other traders heightens my anxiety.

It is one minute before the news is scheduled to be released. I quickly check my equipment. My trading platform is open and ready. My analytical software is receiving data; everything is primed and set for battle. I generally execute two Fed trades. One of them is executed shortly after the news is released. I am in and out of this trade quickly. For that reason, I call it my "Corvette Trade." Only highly experienced traders should take this trade. After I make some quick cash with the Corvette, I let traders digest the news and react rationally to it. Around 2:00 PM, I analyze prices again and reenter the market. That is, I do so if I see a trend and an opportunity. I call this trade the Model "T" because it is a much slower trade. Also, like the original Model "T," it is pretty reliable because I have plenty of time for analysis. I may stay with this trade until the end of the session at 3:15 PM.

My record of success on Fed Day is good—not perfect, but very good. I generally walk away with money in my pockets. I am able to do so because I have a strategy and I know how to execute it properly. Unlike many others, I do not guess the action the Fed will take, and I do not guess the market's reaction to a cut or an increase in rates. I watch prices and let the market lead the way. I just follow.

THE CORVETTE TRADE

On Fed Day, I feel like a kid waiting for Santa on Christmas. If I am patient and read the tape correctly, I will receive a gift, compliments of Bernanke. Around 1:00 PM, I begin to actively prepare for the trade by taking a break from the numbers and action of the market. I step away from the computer and walk around the office for a few minutes, get a cup of coffee or a soda, and spend a few minutes talking with students or employees. I want to feel relaxed and reset my brain to zero. I do not want to approach this trade with any bias. Around 1:10 PM I return to my desk and focus on the numbers. I look at the futures indexes. Prices are bouncing up and down like a kid on a pogo stick. By this time, many traders are anticipating the announcement and placing their bets. I say they are betting because that is exactly what they are doing. They have no more knowledge about what the Fed will do than the rest of us. And even if they knew what action the Fed was going to take, there is no way anyone can predict the reaction of the markets. Nevertheless, these trigger-happy traders foolishly jump in.

At 1:14 PM, one minute before the news should be released, I begin writing down prices. I write them down so I can refresh my memory at a glance. Specifically, I need to know the price of the S&P 500 futures, the Nasdaq 100 futures, and Dow 30 futures, and the Dax futures. Lately, I have also been closely following the Dow Jones EuroStoxx. Per the exchange, this index contains 50 stocks billed as "supersector leaders" from across Europe. On April 30, 2008, the numbers were as follows when I jotted them down:

S&P 500	1400.00
Nasdaq 100	1950.00
Dow 30	12950.00
Dax	7000.00

Those prices are important because they represent the value that traders around the world are placing on these specific investments prior to the news. Once the news is known, if prices move up and break above my numbers, I will take a long position. If they move down and break below them, I will go short. Not only will I use the numbers on this date, but I will use them as benchmarks from today until the next Fed Day. If prices are moving up and approaching those numbers, there will be some resistance there. If prices are going down, expect some support to step in near those prices. Therefore, these price points are important pivot numbers for my near-term trading.

These numbers are so important that I track them on a chart. I write down prices on each of the Seven Sisters. These are so important that I refer to them over and over again in the days that follow the Fed news. Figure 8.1 is the key number chart for April 30, 2008. The numbers on the chart are for Fed Day exclusively. I track the daily open, high, low, the 1:15 PM price and the daily close.

At precisely 1:15 PM on April 30, 2008, the decision is known. For a few moments on this date, the markets seemed confused. I did not see a play until 1:16 and I stayed out. I cautioned my listening audience that I thought

7 Sisters	30-Apr				
	Open	High	Low	Close	1:15pm
ES	1388.00	1407.00	1383.50	1384.50	1400.00
YM	12808	13008	12784	12807	12950
NQ	1939.00	1960.50	1916.75	1923.00	1950.00
DAX	6939.00	7014.00	6895.00	6895.00	6990.00
Crude	115.500	116.700	113.300	114.875	114.150
Gold	871.7	876	862.4	875.6	864.3
Bond	116.059	117.079	115.220	117.059	116.030

FIGURE 8.1 I chart prices just seconds before the Fed news is released. These numbers are very important, and I use them as support, resistance, and pivot prices for weeks.

FIGURE 8.2 A one-minute chart of the E-mini on April 30, 2008. I made the trade, but due to the fast move and shift of prices, I was only able to make about $33.50 per E-mini contract. I was in and out of the action in less than one minute. Some Corvettes pay me more. In fact, most do so, but every trade cannot and will not be a big winner. That is the reality of the market.

this trade would be a fast and furious one. Then prices headed south. I did not need to know what action the Fed took. I can learn that later. What I needed to know was that my sell numbers had been hit and I went short. My trade was a sell on the E-mini S&P at 1398.00. Knowing the potential for a rapid shift in prices, I placed an order to exit my positions at 1396.00 but saw prices shifting and quickly liquidated. On this particular day, I got some slippage. *Slippage* is a term that refers to the difference in the price of the order that was placed and the fill price. I did not make a king's ransom on the trade, but I picked up a few bucks and certainly did not lose a dime. The trade did not work out as well as I would have liked, but I trade multiple contracts and was satisfied with my Corvette. Figure 8.2 shows the rapid Corvette.

Moments after getting out of the trade, the ranks of the bulls swelled and prices went up. I did not take the bait. I moved to the sidelines to wait for the markets to calm down and show their real direction. That was a wise decision because the up move did not last long and I was able to go short again on my Model "T."

THE MODEL "T"

At 2:00 PM, I take another look at prices. If prices are continuing to trend in the direction of the Corvette, I execute another trade. If the Corvette was a short, I want prices still moving below those benchmark levels that I recorded moments before the Fed announcement. With that confirmation, I take another short position. On April 30, 2008, that is exactly what I did. I traded the Dow futures and went short at 12,889. I quickly took a couple of points of profit from part of the position and held the remainder. I exited the last of my Model "T" contracts at 12,836 for a gain in the mini Dow futures of more than 50 points per contract. Figure 8.3 is a five-minute Dow futures chart that shows the Model "T" trade on April 30, 2008.

Remember to exercise a great deal of caution when trading Fed news. Prices may move quickly, and if you are on the wrong side of the action, it is easy to lose thousands of dollars in nothing flat. Only experienced traders who have the skills to exit positions quickly should try this maneuver.

Another example of this trade in action is March 18, 2008. On that date there was a great deal of speculation about the Fed's action. Truth is that there is always a good deal of conjecturing, but with the mortgage crisis in the news and with the Bear Stearns fiasco in the forefront, traders expected a huge cut, and many wanted no less than a full point of relief. The Fed

FIGURE 8.3 A five-minute chart of the Dow futures during the Model "T" on April 30, 2008.

7 Sisters	18-Mar Open	High	Low	Close	1:15pm
ES	1281.50	1334.50	1278.75	1334.00	1305.50
YM	11997	12409	11988	12405	12187
NQ	1696.25	1772.75	1694.50	1771.00	1729.00
DAX	6272.00	6484.50	6270.00	6484.50	6375.50
Crude	106.000	109.925	105.650	109.420	106.225
Gold	1004.8	1013.4	977.2	1004.6	999.2
Bond	120.059	120.084	118.300	119.130	119.260

FIGURE 8.4   Chart of prices just moments before the Fed announcement on March 18, 2008.

responded with a 0.75-basis-point cut. That is a nice reduction in rates, but the market was not satisfied. Initially, prices dropped on the news. That is just a reminder that one cannot guess the market's response to economic information. The immediate play was a short.

After reason and calm returned and the bears stopped partying, the bulls stepped back into the market and took the market up. The Dow rose 420 points and enjoyed the single biggest day gain it had seen in five years.

Figure 8.4 lists the Seven Sisters and the important prices on March 18, 2008.

The March 18, 2008, trade is shown in the chart in Figure 8.5. The Model "T" was a buy, and at DTI we enjoyed riding the prices up.

FIGURE 8.5   A 15-minute chart of the E-mini S&P futures on March 18, 2008.

Trading the Fed is exciting and, for me, profitable. As I prepare for each of those FOMC meetings, I feel like I am waiting for Santa to slide down the chimney. It is a trade that I anticipate with visions of dollar signs in my head. You, too, are invited to watch me trade live on the DTI chat. Just visit www.dtitrader.com on Fed day and see the show.

PEARL 13

The Model "T" provides opportunities to trade stock, futures, and options for three days after the Fed announcement.

REVIEW

Various news events offer traders the chance to make money. One of the biggest regularly scheduled news events is the Fed news. Due to the important role that the Federal Reserve plays in regulating monetary policy, their actions have tremendous consequences. One of the most powerful tools available to them is their ability to set the Federal funds rate. This rate is important to industry, business, and consumers because it determines the cost of borrowing money. Therefore, when rate changes are made, the markets respond.

I generally make two Fed trades. The first is the Corvette Trade, and it is made immediately following the news at 1:15 PM. This is a quick trade and I am in and out of it in minutes and maybe seconds. I trade multiple contracts and plan to average a few points of profit from each contract. I may leave money on the table but my goal is to take some money out of the market for myself. Once the initial surge is over, I am out of the action and on the sidelines.

I wait until 2:00 PM before making my second trade, the Model "T." By the time the Model "T" is executed, traders have had about 45 minutes to evaluate the news and respond in a more rational way to it. I analyze prices using the benchmarks described in this chapter. Then I respond appropriately. I may keep this trade until the exchange closes at 3:15 PM.

CHAPTER 9

Dancing with the Dax

For almost a decade, I have enjoyed dancing with the Dax. The Dax 30 is a powerful German equity index that is comprised of 30 blue-chip German stocks. The shares are traded on the Frankfurt exchange. I trade the futures index and it trades on the Eurex Exchange. My love affair with the Dax began on September 11, 2001, when our financial markets and our nation suffered a brief but major hit. Shortly after the two hijacked jetliners flew into the Twin Towers, U.S. exchanges, including the New York Stock Exchange (NYSE) and the Chicago Mercantile Exchange (CME), shut down and stayed closed for a week. On that fateful Tuesday, I was teaching a class at my trading school in Mobile, Alabama. My students and I were long the S&P 500 futures. I was not watching the news; I was trading and teaching, but I knew from the behavior of the market that something had happened to spook them. Prices began falling quickly and were reacting in a manner that was not typical for the time of day. My students and I had already taken profits from our trade and had a protective stop in place on the remainder of our original position. Our stop was hit as prices headed south, and we were removed from the market.

Realizing that prices were reacting as if some news event had occurred, I asked Geof Smith, our chief instructor, to do a little investigation and report back to us. Geof stepped out of the room and turned on a television in a nearby office. Then he walked back into the room and reported the unbelievable news. We turned on the television in the classroom and watched as further tragic events unfolded. Like the rest of America and much of the world, my students and I were stunned and saddened by the life-changing events that occurred that day.

As a professional trader, with New York and Chicago shut down, I needed to locate a market that was active. It was important to have the ability to hedge positions and execute trades during this time of crisis. After all, I am a trader and my market skills put food on the table and money in the bank. Therefore, I began searching for a foreign stock or futures exchange that was operating. I looked to Asia and tried my hand at trading the Hang Seng in Hong Kong and the Nikkei in Tokyo. My initial attempts were not profitable. Then, when our friends across the Atlantic started trading, I shifted to Europe and focused on the Dax. The Dax paid me, and I continued trading it and making money. Today, the Dax is one of my favorite trading vehicles; I trade it almost every day. I also use it to gauge market sentiment. Over the last few years, I have seen the power of the Dax. I no longer consider taking a trade without using it as an indicator. It is one of the Seven Sisters that were discussed in Chapter 4. The Dax futures trade electronically and open at 1:00 AM and continue to trade until 3:00 PM central time.

When you are trading a product—whether it is a futures contract, a stock, an option, precious metals, or anything else—one of the most important steps that you need to take is to observe the product trade. I began doing just that. Day and night, I watched the Dax, or at least my trading software watched it for me. The RoadMap™ software records prices every 30 minutes and generates a variety of charts as requested. When my eyes were away from the computer screen, the RoadMap™ continued to do my job for me. Then I studied the information. I located times during the 24-hour day when the Dax was most active. I identified key numbers. I did my homework and my analysis. Only then was I ready to formulate some strategies for trading this index.

The Dax is short for Deutsche Aktien Xchange 30. The companies listed on the Dax are some of Germany's biggest. Germany is Europe's largest economy, so the health of this index says a great deal about the German economy and the economies of other parts of Europe and the world. The Dax futures trade in 0.50 increments and the value of each point is 25 euros. The current rate of exchange means that each point is worth about $38 in the United States. Currently, the average daily range exceeds well over 100 points. That wide range offers a number of profit-taking opportunities for me.

Because I always consider risk first, I urge you to do the same. The Dax is one of my personal favorites. However, prices may move quickly. Those on the wrong side of a move may be taken to the cleaners. Before trading, do a great deal of observation. Identify key numbers and important times. Learn about futures in general and the risk involved in them. Trade only when you understand the risk, can afford it, and have a tested strategy. Like our Nasdaq, the Dax is an entirely electronic exchange.

THE EARLY RISER

My favorite time to trade the Dax is between 5:00 and 7:00 AM. I take this trade often—almost every day. I get the Dax range during the first two hours of trading. That is, I need to know the the high and the low from 1:00 to 3:00 AM. At 5:00 AM, I look to determine whether prices are above or below that range. If above the high of the range, I go long; if below, I go short. Figure 9.1 depicts the Dax movement on April 25, 2008.

The range between 1:00 and 3:00 AM extended from a low of 6894 to a high of 6947.50. I wait for a break out of that range. On this date, that breakout came before 5:00 AM, but prices really shot up around 7:00 AM.

At this particular time of day, many statistical indicators like the NYSE issues and tick are not available. Therefore, for confirmation of my play, I

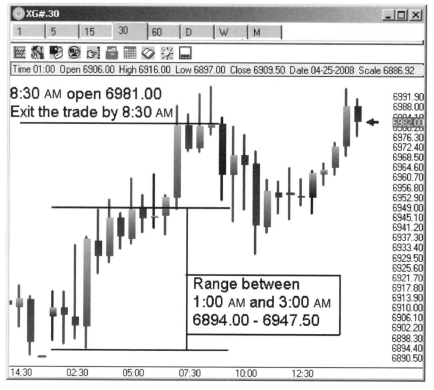

FIGURE 9.1 A 30-minute chart of the Dax futures on April 25, 2008. I use the price range between the open at 1:00 AM central time and 3:00 AM. I wait for a break out of that range and trade in the direction of the break.

use my V-factor, an indicator that gauges volume. If I am short, I want to see sellers coming into the market, and if I am long, I want to see buyers stepping up to the plate. I also get a warm, fuzzy feeling when other European indexes are moving in my direction. Specifically, I look at the FTSE, CAC, and SMI exchanges.

Again, like when making Dow trades, my personal rule is that I buy on the ones and sell on the nines. Once in the trade, I take some quick profits on a portion of my positions. However, if the move seems strong, I may hold a few contracts until just before the United States begins its day session at 8:30 AM central time.

PEARL 14

The 6:00 AM price on the Dax futures is the most important price in the Dax for that day of trading. It may be used as a pivot to gauge whether the overall market should be up or down for the session.

THE BASKETBALL TRADE

It is said that the most important time during a basketball game is the last two minutes of play. On a day when the S&P futures, Nasdaq, and Dow futures are trending in one direction, the most important time for me with the Dax tends to be the last 10 minutes of the session. This trade is based on the same principle as the Face Peel in Chapter 6. The S&P session comes to a close at 3:15 PM, but the Dax, like the NYSE, closes at 3:00 PM.

If the futures indexes have been trending up or down throughout most of their session and the opposing side has been unable to reverse the trend near the close, I buy or sell the Dax at 2:50 PM and ride it for profits for only 10 minutes. That is, if the day's move has been up and the bears cannot gain control as the session winds down, I go long and pick up some points for a short 10-minute run. The reverse is also true. If the trend is down and the bulls are too weak to make a reversal, I sell the Dax at 2:50 PM and ride down for 10 minutes. Figure 9.2 depicts this trade on April 28, 2008. From 2:50 PM until the Dax closed at 3:00 PM, prices dropped nine points. At 25 euros or $38 per point, that represents almost $350 in value per contract.

Remember that trading is an art, and once in a trade, keep your eyes on the indicators and the numbers. If the picture changes and you find yourself on the wrong team, respond appropriately.

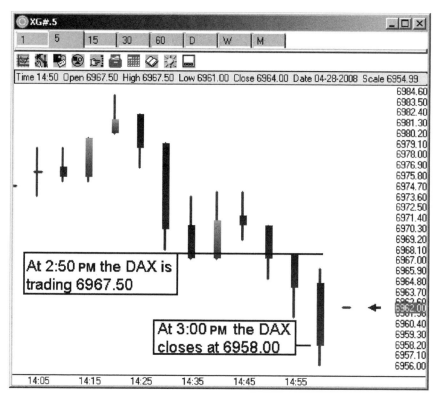

FIGURE 9.2 A five-minute chart of the Dax as it nears its daily close on April 28, 2008.

REVIEW

I enjoy my dance with the Dax. The Dax is a good reflection of global market sentiment, and understanding it will improve your trading with bonds, stocks, and other products. I gain a bit of confidence by using the Dax as a market indicator. Because Germany is Europe's largest economy, the information reflected by the Dax numbers is very important.

I have several trades that I often make on the Dax. I trade early in the morning before the U.S. exchanges open for business. Using the 6:00 AM Dax number, I am able to determine market sentiment and trade with it. Around 10:30 AM, I pay careful attention as the other big exchanges of Europe close their trading pits. Sometimes I execute some positions and ride the wave of those closing to profits. My vehicle is the Dax. Finally, there is another trade that I anticipate regularly. Both the NYSE and the

Dax futures close at 3:00 PM. If I see a trend going into the close, I trade the Dax and ride it for the last 10 minutes before the pits in New York close.

In addition to these trades, I am always looking for new opportunities and ways to make money. To learn more about the Dax futures, visit the Eurex Exchange web site at www.eurexchange.com. If you're interested in educational courses or seminars, contact DTI at www.dtitrader.com.

PEARL 15

Be open-minded and continue to learn.

CHAPTER 10

Money Never
Sleeps

More than two decades ago, I worked for a brokerage house where the bull was all but idolized. Being a team player and a good employee, I followed the "bullish" philosophy, but found myself losing money far too often. Going long is simply not always the right thing to do to make money. I knew that I needed a product that allowed me to be profitable in both up and down markets. Traders who limit their trading to only long positions are very limited in their ability to adapt and trade when economic hard times come and the bears rule. I was considering this problem and looking for a solution when the Chicago Mercantile Exchange (CME) announced that they were introducing a new product, the S&P 500 index futures.

I knew that I needed to trade the S&P, and I immediately did so. Initially, the contract offered was a big contract that traded for $500 per point. A few years later, the contract split, and today it trades for $250 per point. A short time after being introduced, the product line was again expanded with the debut of the E-mini. The E-mini is valued at $50 per point. The lower point value makes this product more appealing to a wider audience of traders. Today, the S&P futures are one of the most frequently traded futures contracts, with over a million contracts traded on the average business day. The volume of activity makes this a great place for day traders to make money. With so many buyers and sellers, it generally only takes a click of the mouse to buy or sell. Also, there is sufficient price movement during the course of the average day to allow for plenty of profits to be made. At the time of this writing, the average true range (ATR) of the E-mini S&P is 20 points, representing a monetary value of $1000 per contract for the total average daily move. The ATR constantly changes, so it is a good idea to regularly verify the daily range. One good site for doing so is www.barcharts.com.

In the early days, the only way to trade the S&P futures was by phoning orders to the floor of the exchange for execution. Business was conducted only when the open outcry pits were active. The Globex terminal changed all of that. In 1987, the CME proposed the concept of an after-hours trading platform, an electronic trading system for futures contracts. However, it took another five years before the ideas were transformed into reality. Now it is possible to trade the S&P almost 24 hours a day. The Globex session opens on Sunday afternoon at 5:00 PM, and on weekdays the action begins at 3:30 PM. Trading continues until 3:15 PM the following day. That means that a regular Globex trading session extends from Monday afternoon to Tuesday afternoon with only a 15-minute gap.

I regularly trade the after-hours markets, and the S&P 500 is one of my venues for making money. Another one of my favorites is the Dax. Because I discuss Dax strategies in Chapter 9, I will focus on S&P plays here. Below are two of the S&P trades that I make on a regular basis.

THE FOLLOW-THROUGH

This trade takes advantage of the movements in the session that has just ended. It is a trade that I execute around 7:00 PM. The first trigger for this trade is a daily Trading Index (TRIN) that closes higher than 2. You will remember from Chapter 4 that the TRIN is a statistical indicator. It measures advances and declines and adds volume to the mix. This indicator is a contrarian indicator that measures the strength and depth of market momentum. To learn more about the TRIN, refer to Chapter 4. Suffice it here to say that a TRIN reading of 2 or greater is very negative. I consider a 2 at the close of the daily session to be a signal that a reversal or correction to some degree may be attempted in after-hours trading. Therefore, rather than looking for a selling opportunity, I look for a buying one.

However, I do not buy until I have some confirmation that my hunch may be correct. There are two things that I check. First, I look for some positive movement in night trading on the S&P, Nasdaq, and Dow futures. Has the downward dive from the day session been halted? Obviously, if these exchanges are continuing to move down and follow the end-of-the-day trend, I will not be a buyer. The bears are too strong and the market is continuing its downward slide.

Another way I look for confirmation for a buy is via the action in Asia. Once the Nikkei in Tokyo and the Hang Seng in Hong Kong open, I check to see how they are trading. Are prices going up or down? If both the U.S. equity index futures and those two Asian products are bullish, I look for a spot to join the bulls. I identify my exact buying position by checking key numbers and identifying support and resistance levels. I do not buy just ahead of major resistance. That would be foolish. But once I identify a good entry point, I click the mouse.

This is a short-term play for me, and I stay with it for only an hour or so. Sometimes I may enter and exit this trade within a 30-minute time span.

The big idea behind this play is that often the day may end down, but the night market may attempt to pull prices back up. It is true that in a truly down market, the bears may rule the day and the night. But there may still be some chances for making some quick profits by going long. Based on the trade criteria, it is obvious that opportunities for this trade do not come around often. But when the setup is present, this may be a good trade. When taking such a trade, be sure you have the skills to manage your money and exit trades quickly. Prices move much slower at night than during the day, and one may think erroneously that the odds of losing money are, therefore, less. That is not necessarily true. It is possible to lose money after hours. Be careful with your trading. Use stop/loss strategies and understand risk.

TRADING WHEN THE SUN RISES

Another S&P trade that I make is an early-morning trade. After getting a good night's rest, I step to my computer a little before 6:00 AM and review the markets. I am anxious to see if there has been any unexpected action while I was resting. I am especially interested in taking a look at the Dax futures. I use the Dax index both as a trading vehicle and as a market indicator. If the mood in German is gloomy, that pessimistic outlook will be reflected in the Dax. The reverse will also be true. Positive views of the financial markets will send prices on the Dax upward. Therefore, a quick check of Dax prices gives me a general view of market sentiment across the Atlantic. Since its open, is the Dax trading up or down?

After identifying the sentiment in Europe, I look at the V-Factor. This indicator works 24 hours a day and is a volume indicator. By this time of the morning, the V-Factor has had more than 15 hours to collect data for Globex trading. S&P opened its Globex at 3:30 PM on the previous afternoon. If the V-Factor is registering a reading that is lower than 0.70, I start looking for an opportunity to short the market because the V-Factor is telling me that the bears are stronger than the bulls. I will short the S&P E-mini. Again, this may be a brief play. Sometimes I am in the trade for only a few minutes, and other times I may hold the position until nearly 8:00 AM—just in front of the opening of the day-trading session in the United States.

TRADING AFTER-HOURS NEWS

Another way that I use the after-hours market is to trade early-morning news. Since I have already devoted a chapter to news, I will just briefly explain the role of the Globex and early news. Many big news events are released at 7:30 AM. The open outcry pits are closed at the time. However, by using the Globex, it is possible to trade the equity index futures and make money. Figure 10.1 shows a trade that was made on May 2, 2008.

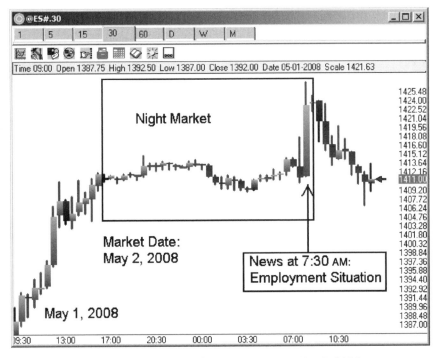

FIGURE 10.1 A 30-minute chart of the E-mini S&P on May 2, 2008.

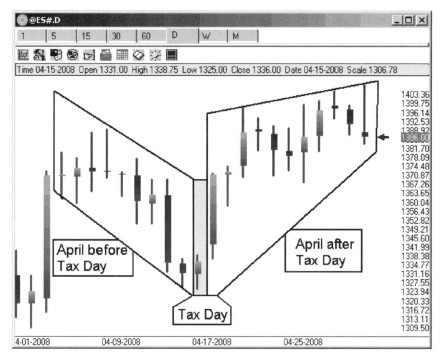

FIGURE 10.2 A daily chart of April showing how prices on the E-mini S&P futures reacted in 2008 to Tax Day.

Employment numbers were released. Prices shot up in response to the numbers. I did not have to wait for 8:30 AM to make my play. As Figure 10.2 shows, I traded the E-mini S&P and made money.

HOLIDAY TRADING

Not only is it possible to trade the S&P futures after hours, but it is also possible to do so on many holidays when the pits on trading floors in Chicago and New York are empty. For example, the CME is open Thanksgiving morning and is also conducting business as usual the week between Christmas and New Year's. Folks who know me, are probably not surprised to learn that I am one of the individuals who will likely be sneaking away from the feast and festivities to execute a trade at Thanksgiving. Admittedly, volume is thin, but that is what I enjoy. I know that if the bulls start charging; the bears will be nowhere in sight. Or if the bears emerge from their caves, the bulls will be grazing at grandmother's house. That means that I usually enjoy a slow-trending market that pays me.

PEARL 16

Thanksgiving Day tends to have one of largest percentage up days of the year.

Throughout the year, there are certain holidays that seem to have significance for the markets. Some of these include Tax Day (April 15), Memorial Day, July 4th, Labor Day, Thanksgiving, and Christmas. Often, as the new year begins, there is enthusiasm and an attempt to move prices higher. If the bulls succeed, the upward trend may continue for a couple of months. In April, the taxman comes calling, and there is often a trend reversal. Having to write those checks to Uncle Sam deflates the spirits and the pocketbooks of many investors. Memorial Day is another big holiday of significance. The Memorial Day weekend marks the official start of the summer holidays. As the temperature rises around the United States, volume is light, the markets are dull, and trading is difficult. During much of this time, the only play that will pay is selling on strength and buying on weakness. With thin volume, there may be a trend reversal. July 4th may usher in a bit of excitement, but other than that, the summer doldrums will probably continue until Labor Day. Labor Day marks the official end of summer vacation, and traders get back to work. Initially, prices may bump up. However, historically, following Labor Day, the market weakens until the Thanksgiving turkey starts strutting again on the horizon.

PEARL 17

The week of December 26 through January 1 is the best trading week of the year.

To maximize profit-making opportunities, learn about seasonal markets. Check trading hours by visiting the CME web site or other relevant exchange sites. Having that knowledge will allow you to take advantage of general trends. Obviously, the same trends and patterns do not always develop. However, they often do, and anticipating them can be profitable. For the holiday schedules for 2008, go to www.cme.com and view the calendar.

Market Generalizations for Consideration

January 1	Traders begin the year with enthusiasm and generally try to push prices higher.
April 15	Tax Day ushers in gloom and doom. A trend may be reversed.
Memorial Day	Beginning of summer, and volume falls as temperatures rise.
July 4th	Enthusiasm returns as traders anticipate the holiday. However, the excitement will likely be short-lived as volume soon evaporates.
Labor Day	Official end of summer, and volume returns.
Thanksgiving	Enthusiasm again returns, and the markets tend to rally through the Christmas season.
Christmas	A happy time when markets often rally.

Jeff Hirsch, the author of the *Stock Trader's Almanac* (published by John Wiley & Sons) gives specifics that allow the new trader as well as the old trader to increase his odds of success by knowing the details of history and explaining the connections of time and price. For information about how the calendar affects trading, go to www.stocktradersalmanac.com. Perhaps the *Almanac* can also be a useful tool for you.

Figure 10.2 depicts the frequent reaction to trading in early mid-April. Tax Day tends to be important to traders and to the markets.

PEARL 18

The market usually reverses its trend after July 4th.

AFTER HOURS—A NEW FRONTIER

Few careers offer as much flexibility as trading. With a computer and Internet access, trading is a mobile vocation. In fact, you can board a virtual train and travel around the world electronically to trade foreign markets without stepping a foot out of your home on Main Street. Or you can spend your days golfing while using your nights for trading. Today's trader can even trade on many holidays. The opportunities are endless because revolutions in technology and communications have expanded the universe.

After-hours trading is valuable for several reasons. First, electronic markets increase the hours and the products that you can trade. In the 1980s, I could not have imagined that today I would have the capability to trade a German index from my home in Mobile, Alabama, at 2:00 AM. I am living proof that after-hours markets expand opportunities.

Second, information gained from after-hours markets is valuable and can improve one's trading during the regular day's session. Before I place my first trade in the morning, I know the world's sentiment. I check the prices on major indexes across Asia and Europe. During their most recent trading sessions, were traders around the world bullish or bearish? Once I gain that information, I am then able to use it to make more enlightened trading decisions when the pits in New York and Chicago open for business. If the world is bearish, I want to think long and hard before taking on a long position.

Finally, after-hours markets are great places to hedge positions or trade after-hours news. For example, if a major world event occurs after the trading pits are closed, an after-hours trader can log in to his platform and buy or sell as needed to hedge his portfolio. Or he can trade to take advantage of the news. If the news is viewed by the world to be significantly positive, the markets will respond and soar upward. After-hours traders can profit from the move. Or, if bad news is aired, the effects of the disaster will be reflected in the futures after-hours markets. Those who know how to maximize their trading can go short and make money. However, one must be prepared in advance. Once a market-moving event occurs, it is too late to open an account or learn the ropes. Be prepared to react before a crisis or exceptional event occurs.

CHARACTERISTICS OF NIGHT MARKETS

If you have never traded after hours, be sure to observe the market before putting any money at risk. Prices during the night session may move at a snail's pace. There have been times when I have placed my orders in the early afternoon, gone to dinner, watched a little television, and then stepped to my computer to check on my trade. At that time I learned that the order was not yet filled because prices had not moved. On other occasions, prices might be very active. For example, during earnings season, a blue-chip company may energize markets or some other event may get prices hopping.

On slow-moving nights, traders may have the feeling that there is reduced risk. That is not true. It is always possible to lose money when trading. Always consider risk, trade when the odds for success are on your side, and manage your money.

A bit of information that might be helpful to know is that DTI and brokersXpress are currently working on a joint project for automated trading after hours. You can check this out at www.dtitrader.com.

REVIEW

The financial markets are at your fingertips virtually 24 hours a day. Learn about trading around the clock and use technology and knowledge to make money. Two of my favorite after-hours venues are the Dax and the S&P futures. Dax trading is discussed in Chapter 9. I also enjoy trading the S&P during the night and early morning hours. Two of my favorite trades are the follow-through, a trade that takes advantage of the momentum of the day's session that has just ended, (a reversal play) and an early-morning trade, an S&P play that I make during the Globex session. I use the Dax 6:00 AM price; the V-Factor, a proprietary volume indicator; and the aggregate sentiment across Asia and Europe to make this play.

After-hours trading not only opens the door for making money at night and in the early-morning hours, but it also allows traders to access the financial markets during many holidays when the trading pits are closed. By using electronic exchanges that operate virtually around the clock, it is possible to expand the hours available for trading, trade on holidays, hedge positions, and just make more money.

CHAPTER 11

Cashing in on Bonds

C ontinuing education is powerful. As you learn more, you are able to trade more products and do so with a greater level of success. I have traded bonds for 25 years, but my success level was not as great as I would have liked. I never had a strategy that allowed me to trade bonds often. Therefore, trading bonds was not part of my daily routine. Then, in early 2008, that changed when I read an article in *Futures* magazine. The article was about trading bonds and offered some helpful information. I took the ideas presented and merged them with my knowledge about the S&P and the markets. For the first time, I am enjoying trading bonds because I am consistently making money with the trade. Now bond trading has become a daily staple for me, and it is a steady moneymaker.

Bonds are debt instruments; that means they are interest rate sensitive. The buyer of the bond expects to receive repayment of his principal with interest. When interest rates move up, bond prices move down. For example, if interest rates are 5 percent and move up to 6 percent, bond prices drop. Who wants to buy a 5 percent bond if he can get one that pays 6 percent? Therefore, bonds carrying a lower rate must be sold at a discount. At the time of this writing, the Federal Open Market Committee (FOMC) has been lowering rates for months. While rates have been dropping steadily, bond prices have also been dropping. In a healthy economy, interest rates tend to rise as the economy grows, but our economy has not been robust lately and that fact is reflected in our interest rates and prices in the bond market.

Bonds tend to move inversely to stocks. One example of this can be seen on May 2, 2008. The morning began with the release of employment

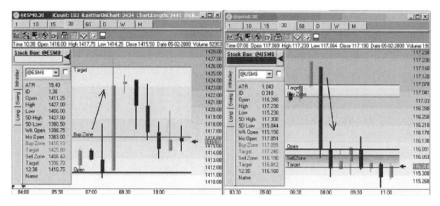

FIGURE 11.1 Both charts are 30-minute charts showing how prices responded to some good news on May 2, 2008. The S&P equity index futures shot up and the bond futures took a nosedive.

numbers. The employment situation was reported at 7:30 AM central time by the U.S. Department of Labor. The governmental agency had expected dire numbers, but the information was not nearly as bad as expected. There was an increase in nonagricultural employment. As employment goes up, there are fewer applicants in the job pool and employers are forced to pay higher wages. Increased wages spur inflation. Bonds markets do not like inflation. Therefore, in response to the news on May 2, 2008, the S&P went up but bonds moved down in price. Figure 11.1 depicts this relationship. The chart on the right is a 30-minute S&P E-mini chart. Notice that when news was released, the S&P shot up. An arrow points to the upward move of the equity index on the good news. The chart on the left is bond futures. It is also a 30-minute chart and shows the response of the bond market to the news. Bond prices fell quickly in unison with the upward jump of the S&P.

I trade the 30-year Treasury bond. The symbol for this bond is US, and it is traded at the CME Group on the Globex. This bond trades in 1/64ths, and each 64th is valued at $15.63, for a total value per point of $1000. I make my bond trade after the first hour of trading. The bond pit opens at 7:20 AM central time. I observe for one full hour. Then I note the high and low during that hour. I use that one hour of trading as a reference bar. I am looking for a break above the high or below the low. If I see a break, I check the S&P futures for confirmation, and if I get that confirmation, I make the trade. If bonds are going up, the S&P should be going down, and vice versa. Figure 11.2 is a chart of the bond trade on April 22, 2008. Geof Smith, our chief instructor, as well as some of our students, made the trade on that date.

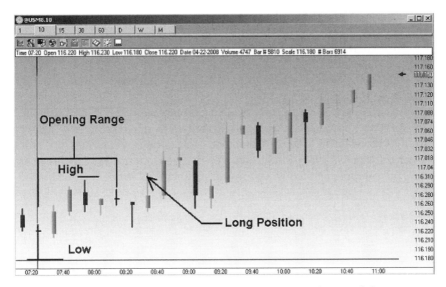

FIGURE 11.2 The upward path of bonds after prices broke out of the range established during the first hour of trading. The chart is a 10-minute chart on April 22, 2008.

There is a wide array of financial products to trade. If you have the knowledge, it is possible to make money on many fronts. Thanks to that article in *Futures* magazine and the DTI method, I have been able to increase my moneymaking potential.

REVIEW

Bonds are another way to make money in the markets. At the time of this writing, I have one bond trade that I make often. In order to trade bonds successfully, it is necessary to understand some basic facts. Bonds are debt instruments, and interest rates and inflation affect bond prices. When interest rates go up, bond prices come down. Also, there tends to be an inverse relationship between stocks and bond prices. The chart in Figure 11.1 graphically illustrates this relationship. As the S&P equity index futures are going up, bonds are selling off. The bars are almost identical, but in reverse direction.

I use the first hour of bond trading to establish some benchmark prices. When prices go above the high of the range of the first hour of trading, I go long; when prices fall below the low of that first hour, I go short. It seems very simple. At the time of this writing, this simple strategy has worked over and over again for my students and me.

My experience with trading bonds highlights one of the important things about trading. Trading and the trades that are successful are always changing as the market changes. Dynamic markets mandate dynamic strategies.

Also, as new knowledge is gained, you are better able to understand the markets and design trades and strategies to make money. A strategy that works well today or for a number of months or years may not work under different market conditions. For that reason, traders have to learn from the markets and adapt and tweak strategies as needed.

CHAPTER 12

Options Strategies to Make Money

I have traded options for many years. You will recall that it was an options trade that caused me great grief in October 1987. Even though I still trade options, I use a different approach. That is, I respect risk and make much smaller, safer trades. Today, I am far wiser and would never dream of trading 1000 or so naked options. The gray on my head attests to the wisdom I have gained as each year has passed.

An option is a contract that gives the owner the right but not the obligation to engage in a future transaction of an underlying security at a specified price on or before a specified date. The option contract may be executed if the underlying security reaches the specified price or strike price set forth in the contract. For example, if the strike price for an option is $35, when the per-share stock price reaches the magic $35 mark, the strike price has been hit. If the option has not expired, the contract may be executed.

Options are unlike most other financial products in that options expire if they are not exercised. Options contracts for equities expire on the third Friday of their expiration month. The contract must be executed on or before the date specified in the contract. If the option is not executed on or before the expiration date, it becomes useless and is null and void.

There are two big categories or types of options: calls and puts. A call is a contract that allows the buyer to "call" the stock away from the seller at a specified price or strike price. For example, if someone buys an October 35 GE call, he has the right to "call" the stock away from the seller at the strike price of $35. If the strike price is hit, the call allows the buyer to obtain the stock at that price. A put is a contract that allows the buyer to "put" the stock to the seller of the contract at a set price or strike price. If someone buys an October 35 GE put, the buyer has the option to sell the stock to the writer or seller of the put when the stock price reaches the strike price.

Each equity option contract controls the right to 100 shares of the underlying stock. Because options give ownership rights in another asset (i.e., stock), an option is a derivative. Derivatives have unique risk, and it is important to know these risks and fully understand them before trading the product. Check with your broker and ask for written materials that specify in detail all of the risks involved.

In order to buy an option, you must pay a premium. The premium is the cost of the option, and that money goes to the seller of the option and will not be returned to you. An option contract price is quoted in dollars and cents. As noted above, most options contracts control 100 shares of the underlying stock. If the price is $1.50, that amount is multiplied by 100. The cost of the option in this example is $150. That is the premium received by the seller of the option.

If the strike price established in the contract is reached or exceeded, the option is said to be "in the money." For example, if you have a September 135 put on Apple, and Apple is trading at $134, the contract is in the money.

The premium is the cost of the option, and it consists of intrinsic value and time value. Intrinsic value is the amount of money a contract is "in the money." Intrinsic value is equal to the share price minus the strike price. (This cannot be negative; if the strike price is higher than the share price, the value will be zero.) Time value is the amount of money a contract is "out of the money." Time value is equal to the premium minus the intrinsic value.

There are short-term and long-term options. Long-term equity anticipation securities (LEAPS) are long-term options and by definition have an expiration date greater than nine months. Due to the length of time involved, these options are affected less by time decay. Most options go out three or four months, but LEAPS go out up to four years. LEAPS expire on the third Friday in January of their expiration year. If LEAPS are held for more than one year, profits from LEAPS are taxed as long-term capital gains.

In order to trade options, you must have a brokerage account and complete an Options Account Agreement and sign a risk disclosure agreement. Many brokers allow for options trading. One such broker is OptionsXpress. If you want to learn more about trading options, check out their web site at www.OptionsXpress.com. Once the application is complete and the risk disclosure read, understood, and signed, the brokerage house will evaluate the application to determine whether options trading will be allowed with the account. If the broker believes that the application merits approval for long positions with limited risk, that portion of the application may be approved. Short positions carry unlimited risk and may not be approved for all applicants. The level of trading that is approved depends on a number of factors, including financial strength and experience. It is possible to trade options on futures contracts, but a futures margin account is needed to do so.

The type of account that you have will determine the type of option strategy that you can play. A cash account allows for trading long options and covered calls. A margin account is required to trade short options and uncovered or naked options. Unlike stocks, long option contracts are not marginable.

Options are far less familiar to most traders than stocks. Therefore, before trading them, do your homework and learn the peculiar characteristics of options and how to use them for your optimum financial advantage. As noted above, acquiring the right to buy or sell is not free. The price of the right is the cost of the premium. The grantor of the option receives the premium, and it is his to keep regardless of whether or not the strike price of the option is hit. Mathematical calculations are made to determine the value of the option and that determines the premium. The price of the option has a lot to do with the price of the underlying security, including the following:

- The current market price of the underlying security.
- The strike price of the option, particularly in relation to the current market price of the underlying security.
- The cost of holding a position in the underlying security, including interest and dividends.
- The time until expiration together with any restrictions on when exercising may occur.
- An estimate of the future volatility of the underlying security's price over the life of the option.

The closer the strike price is to the current trading price of the underlying security, the higher the premium. The seller or writer of the option is taking the risk and he will ask for a higher price because there is a greater likelihood that the strike price will be hit. Conversely, the further the strike price is away from the current price, the lower the premium because there are reduced odds that the strike price will be hit and the option exercised. For example, if IBM is trading at $109 and you want to buy a 110 call, the premium will cost more than a $115 call because the $115 contract is more "out of the money." The chances of the strike price being hit are less. As options move closer to expiration, "out of the money" calls and puts decrease in value. Options that are "in the money" as expiration nears will retain their value.

As noted above, the option premium or cost of the option is made of intrinsic value and time value. If GE is trading at $36 per share, the October 35 call is 2. The intrinsic value is $1 and the time value is $1. Remember that the intrinsic value is the amount of money a contract is in the money. The intrinsic value is equal to the share price ($36) less the strike price ($35). In this example the intrinsic value is $1.

Time value is the amount of money a contract is out of the money. The time value is the premium less the intrinsic value.

There is one final factor that will affect option price and that is volatility. The volatility of the underlying security is important. The more volatile the underlying security, the higher the premium will be. Likewise, the less volatile the underlying security is, the lower the premium will be.

OPTIONS LOGIC AND RISK

When buying a call option, you pay a premium. For that premium, you gain the right to buy the underlying security at the set price when and if the strike price is hit. The maximum risk or amount of money that you can lose is the price of the premium. When buying a call, the assumption is that the stock price will rise. It is best to go long calls 60 to 45 days out from expiration to avoid time decay. As with buying a call, if you buy a put, the maximum exposure is the cost of the premium. Also, as with buying a call, I recommend only going out 60 to 45 days when buying a put.

Going short a call without owning the underlying security is a far riskier proposition. This is known as selling naked calls. If the strike price is hit, you will be forced to sell the security at the strike price and deliver it to the purchaser of the option. The risk is unlimited.

When buying a call option, the buyer pays the seller the premium. When shorting a call, the seller receives the premium. If the strike price is not hit, the seller keeps the premium.

Time decay is a friend to the seller of call options. The seller does not want the call to get to the strike price. It is best to sell call options 30 to 45 days out from expiration and hold them until expiration in order to keep the premium. Going short a put without being short the underlying security is selling a naked put. Like shorting stock, the upside risk can be substantial. When selling a put option, the seller assumes the underlying security will move higher. When purchasing a put option, the buyer pays the seller the premium. When shorting a put option, the seller receives the premium. As long as the underlying security does not get to or exceed the strike price, the seller gets to keep the premium. Time decay is a friend to the seller of the put option. The seller does not want the put to get to the strike price. It is best to sell put options 30 to 45 days out from expiration and hold them until expiration in order to keep the premium. This decreases the probability of the underlying security getting to the strike price.

OPTIONS STRATEGIES

Options are a low cost way to hedge your stock portfolio. The usual way that this is done is by buying puts on an index or exchange-traded fund (ETF). There are many ETFs, and a little research should allow you to identify one that will serve your purpose. Since most stocks move with the indexes, you can buy put options to offset your portfolio and gain some protection from a bearish downturn in the market. Following are some of the ETFs that you might want to consider:

SPY	S&P 500
DIA	Dow 30
QQQQ	Nasdaq 100
XLU	Utility
XLE	Energy
GLD	Gold
SLV	Silver

The strategy is not difficult if you understand some basic information. If your stock portfolio is worth $50,000 in the current market and the market is weak, you may want to do some hedging. You may not want to liquidate your positions but do not want to be left helpless if a major downturn happens. You can use ETFs like the Diamond, which is a Dow 30 fund and short the fund to offset losses in your equity account. By hedging your stock positions, even though you may be losing money with equities, you can devise a strategy to offset all or part of those losses with options. In other words, the stock portion of the portfolio may go down in value but the options valuation may increase so that the overall portfolio valuation is maintained. That is the goal of this strategy.

PROBING

Probing is another way to benefit from options. If you have analyzed the market and believe that prices are moving up or down, you can use options to let your analysis work for you. For example, if you believe that a stock is going to move up in price, you do not need to purchase the stock, just buy the option. You are able to get a low risk trade, finance it, and see if your analysis will pay.

Options May Offer Protection

At DTI, we suggest that you never trade without a stop. Using stop/loss orders offers some protection for a market that misbehaves. However, another way to get protection is by using options. Stocks may gap down and there may be a large amount of slippage. Even with a stop/loss order, a great deal of money may be lost. However, if you have an option, it may be executed at the strike price regardless of the slippage. Some stocks do not have options. If your stocks do, using options may offer an advantage.

An Income-Producing Strategy

A covered call is a short call option position in which the seller of the call owns the underlying stock or security. Covered calls carry less risk. If the strike price is hit and the contract must be executed, the seller of the option simply sells what he already owns. To make money from stock that is already owned, you must first locate one that has a tradable option. Remember that not all stocks have options. A great source for gaining this information is OptionsXpress.

Once the stock is identified and you own the stock you may sell the option for a premium. The premium is cash coming to you that you can keep. If the strike price is not hit, you also keep the stock. If the strike price is hit, you are able to keep the premium but must fulfill the contract by giving up the stock to the owner of the option at the established price. There is clearly less risk associated with this strategy. There are few times in life when you can "have your cake and eat it, too." However, if the strike price is not hit in the above scenario that is exactly the way it works out.

If you try this strategy, it is suggested that you sell calls two months out. Options only go out three months. Sell the option at a point where you feel comfortable about getting out of the stock with a profit. The steps for executing this strategy are:

- Own the stock.
- Sell a call against the stock.
- Collect the premium.
- If the strike price is not hit, keep both the premium and the stock.
- If the strike price is hit, you will keep the premium and also make money on the appreciated price of the stock (the price has gone up to the strike price and you are selling the stock at the higher price to the owner of the option).

REVIEW

Options are yet another way to make money on Wall Street. Options differ from stocks and futures in a number of important ways. Before trading options, learn the terms and logic behind options. The information presented in this chapter is merely a brief introduction to the world of options. Before risking money, understand how options work and all of the risk associated with them.

Once you have a grasp of options, they may be used effectively to achieve several important financial goals. They may be used to hedge your portfolio, to probe the market or to speculate, or they may be used for portfolio protection or crash avoidance. Furthermore, covered calls may be used for additional income generation.

CHAPTER 13

Reaping Profits on the Farm

If I see a juicy piece of low-hanging fruit, I pluck it. When I see a market that is ripe for profits, I move to that arena. That is exactly what I have been doing recently with commodities. As noted previously, I am a trader, and if money can be made buying or selling a product, I am probably trading it. Over the years, I have traded various commodities, including oil and energy, gold and precious metals, pork and beef. Lately, corn has been on my radar screen. Oil prices have been sharply increasing for many months, and that fact has resulted in a new focus on the production of biofuels including ethanol. Corn is one of the agricultural products needed for that technology. With demand rising, stockpiles have also been falling. According to AP business writer Stevenson Jacobs, in April 2008, the U.S. Department of Agriculture predicted that farmers in the United States would plant less corn in 2008 than in the previous year—8 percent less to be exact. Greater demand paired with less supply always translates into price increases, and that has been the case with corn. On April 3, 2008, corn jumped to $6 a bushel—a record high.

The United States is the largest producer of corn in the world, and our strain on supply will have a worldwide effect. As Jacobs explains, corn is not only a U.S. food staple, but corn and corn syrup are also used in a wide array of products. In addition, corn is a major source of feed for livestock. As supplies shrink, the price for a bushel of corn will just keep going up and up, and the effects will ripple throughout the economy and around the world. At the time of this writing, I am long corn. The market is bullish, and I am riding the bull wagon to profits week after week. I am using a strategy that I learned in my early days of trading. That is,

I am using the "Bigger Fool" approach. I learned this particular strategy about three decades ago when I lived in Oklahoma City. The basis of the strategy is simple: Buy a product at a high price, and there is always someone (a Bigger Fool) who will buy it from you at an even higher price. Of course, the strategy works only in strong bullish markets like the current one for corn. Obviously, if prices are falling, it may be difficult to find a "Bigger Fool."

Even when prices are high—especially when they are high—this strategy tends to work well. Prices may seem unrealistically top heavy, but that is the strength of the theory: prices are rising even though the increase may be irrational. The Bigger Fool Theory is based on both reason and emotion. In those early days in Oklahoma, it worked like a charm for me, and it has also been working well in the current bull market for corn. I am making money buying corn at very inflated prices—even at all-time highs. It may seem outrageous to go long at the top, but in this market every day seems to make a new high and my profits just keep rolling in. When I trade corn, I trade corn futures.

A few years ago, I rarely traded corn. Generally, I would get into that particular market only once a quarter. However, at the time of this writing, I find myself trading corn almost daily. There are a couple of reasons for my renewed love of the golden agriculture crop. First, the market is so bullish that it is hard for a trader like me to pass up opportunities to trade it. Second, new technologies make access so easy. No need to call the exchange. Just use the computer and click the mouse. I use the Bigger Fool Theory to trade corn futures at the CME Group. In addition to the Bigger Fool Theory, I also have adapted my Face Peel trade (explained in Chapter 6) to make money in corn.

THE MORNING FACE PEEL

I typically trade corn futures between 5:00 AM and 5:30 AM central time. The electronically traded corn futures open at 6:30 PM and trade until 5:30 AM. At 5:30 AM, when there is a halt in trading for three and a half hours. Then trading resumes electronically, and the trading pits of the exchange are also open for business. Both the electronic session and the open outcry pits close at 1:30 PM. I take advantage of trading during the 30 minutes before the morning trading break. This is generally an active time for corn because traders who have been on the wrong side of the action throughout the evening are exiting their positions or shifting sides before the open outcry pits open.

The trade is simple to execute. I look to see if a trend is in place. Is the market moving in an identifiable direction? If so, I identify that direction and try to find the right entry price for a play. The average night move for corn futures is about 12 cents (at least that is the case at the time of this writing). If there has been a six-cent move from the Globex opening price until that 5:00 AM time frame, I go in the direction of the move. If there has been a six-cent move up, I buy. If there has been a six-cent move down, I sell. In addition to looking for an identifiable trend, I also want confirmation from the agricultural complex. That is, if I am going long, I want to see soybeans and wheat going up, and if I am shorting corn, I want to see those commodities going down. Soybean is the most traded of these three products, so it should be moving in price in the same direction as corn before you enter a position. I will ride the move for that 30-minute time frame before the early-morning break.

The trading symbol for corn is C, and the futures contracts expire every other month. You need a margin account to trade corn, and at this time the good-faith deposit needed to trade a single corn contract is approximately $3000. However, that sum may change from time to time, so it is always necessary to check with your broker for exact requirements. Corn trades in 0.0025 increments like the E-mini S&P futures contract; the value of each tick is $12.50. Four ticks represent a penny of movement, and the value of each penny of movement is $50. In other words, if you are accustomed to trading the S&P E-mini futures, the point value is the same. Figure 13.1 charts corn as it breaks out of the opening trading range. On this particular date, I bought at $616 and sold at $618.

As with all trading, exercise great caution. Watch the market before trading. See how and when corn moves. Identify points of support and resistance. Understand all of the risk involved. Only then will you be ready to venture into this market.

REVIEW

During my trading career, I have traded various commodities. When a particular product starts making the news because supplies are short and demand is high, prices will normally begin moving up. I say "normal" because the supply/demand equation will push prices up unless there is some governmental involvement. When a particular market is ripe for profits, I will probably be trading it. I have traded beef, pork, pork bellies, corn, wheat, and soybeans. I do not trade these commodities every day, but there are times when I shift my attention there and make money.

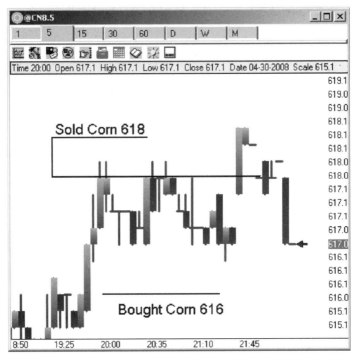

FIGURE 13.1 A five-minute chart of corn futures in the early-morning hours on April 30, 2008.

If the market is extremely bullish and the entire grain complex like wheat and soybeans is also bullish, I will be looking for a price point to make a long play. If the market is strong enough, buying at outrageously high prices can still yield profits when buyers push even higher. If I am trading corn, I usually trade between 5:00 and 5:30 AM. Corn closes for three and a half hours, and I am able to briefly take advantage of the trend that has been set by night and early-morning traders.

CHAPTER 14

Going for the Gold

In 2003, gold began a bullish run that has been sustained for more than four years. I have been bullish on the shiny metal since I spoke to a group of traders and investors in Vegas that year. Up to that time, I had not traded gold for 12 years because I did not see the right play. At the time of this writing, I am long hard metals—not futures. I may day trade futures but my long-term play is with the actual product. The chart in Figure 14.1 tells the gold story. Prices have made a steady move upward over the course of many years. Like all markets, there have been periods of consolidation and short, brief corrections, but the overall trend has been unquestionably up, as Figure 14.1 clearly depicts.

Gold is traded at the Chicago Mercantile Exchange (CME) Group and the Commodity Exchange (COMEX). At the CME, trading begins at 6:16 PM and continues until 4:00 PM the following day. Like the S&P 500 E-mini contract, mini gold is totally electronic. A big gold contract is traded at the COMEX from 9:30 AM until 1:30 PM and trading is conducted in an open outcry pit. At the CME Group, the symbol for mini gold is YG and for the big contract it is ZG. Gold moves in 10-point increments; that is, there are 10 ticks per dollar of movement. Each tick of the mini contract is valued at $3.32 or $33.20 per point of movement. Each tick of the big contract is valued at $10, and the value of a point of movement is $100.

When I am trading gold, I watch the precious metals complex. That is, I watch movement on silver and platinum also. I want all three of these commodities moving in the same direction and confirming my play. If precious metals as a group, are moving up, I may make a day-trade play, but I rarely day trade gold.

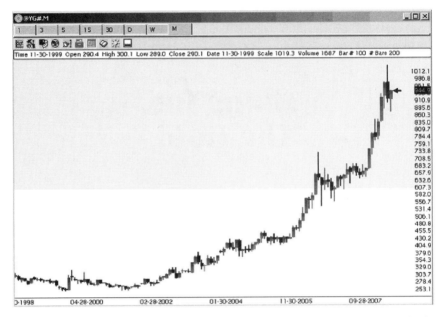

FIGURE 14.1 Gold prices as they have moved up. In 2003, the steady climb began.

Geof Smith, our chief instructor at DTI, is an avid gold trader. Geof enjoys trading gold often and especially trades it in the wake of market-moving news. That means that Geof has many opportunities to trade because gold is highly sensitive to economic news and prices will become very active when economic data is reported. There is usually a big price response to any information about inflation, recession, or deflation. The reason for the extreme sensitivity of gold to news is that gold and precious metals are deemed by many traders and investors to be a safe haven in time of trouble. If other investments are heading south, they put their money in gold for safekeeping. Gold is also very sensitive to inflation fears because it is an international currency that is deemed by investors to hold its value. Investors put their money here in an attempt to preserve the value of their assets.

In 2003, gold was trading around $280 an ounce. At the time of this writing, gold is trading around $940 an ounce and is in a consolidation mode. It has been as high as $1016 an ounce. In late March 2008, it made a new high and immediately corrected to $876 an ounce. Since that tumble, it has gained some ground.

Geof position trades gold. That is, he enjoys swing trading and holding his trades for days, weeks, or even months if he is getting paid. Here is how Geof does it. First, he identifies important key numbers. Gold, just like other trading products, has important support and resistance levels. Begin by studying charts and locating the levels of support and resistance near the current trading price. Study monthly, weekly, and daily charts. Once you have a feel for how gold likes to move and know support and resistance levels, you may want to begin dabbling. It is probably a good idea to try simulations first, and it is always recommended that before trading you study, learn, and observe.

Geof looks for breakouts and buys pullbacks. He trades gold futures. Electronically traded gold futures open at 6:16 PM. Geof generally makes his move between 6:30 and 9:30 PM. Note the opening price and watch movement in relation to that price. If there is a new high, he puts in a buy order at the open. Many times, there is a pullback to the opening price and his order is elected. After returning to the open, prices often continue the original path back up. He follows the same steps for shorting gold.

At the time of this writing, mini gold moves an average of 24 points in a session, which translates into a value of $800 per contract. Always know the average true range (ATR) of anything that you are trading. In that way you are better able to keep expectations in line and identify profit targets and stop/loss placement.

Because Geof swing trades gold, he gives it room to move without hitting his stop with every bobble. If he is long, he puts his initial stop below the previous day's low. If he is short, he puts it above the previous day's high. That means that he is risking about $800 to $1000 per contract. If Geof wants to stay in the trade for a longer period of time, he may use the weekly support and resistance levels for stop placement. That is, if he is long, he may put his stop below the weekly low, and if he is short, the stop/loss order may go above the weekly high. In all markets prices bobble up and down. If you want to stay with a trade for a longer period of time, it is essential to give the market room to move. A brief dip down will occur even in the strongest bull markets, and vice versa. If stops are too tight, money will be lost even if the analysis was right on the money. Once Geof is making money and prices are going his way, he adjusts the stop to lock in profits and reduce risk.

Risk is a very personal issue. For some traders, the risk that Geof takes is too big to take. If they are wrong in their analysis or the market is misbehaving, the stop gets hit and the money is lost. For other folks, that stop is well within their risk tolerance. Remember that risk is personal. Do not take risks that you cannot afford. If there is too much risk involved in a trade, let that trade go. There are many things to trade—stocks, options, commodities, futures—find trades that you can afford and stay away from those that are too rich for your trading pockets.

As noted earlier, gold is highly news sensitive. It is especially vulnerable to Fed news. Therefore, if you are holding a gold position on Fed Day, I suggest you do as Geof does and tighten your stop just before the news announcement. He moves much closer to the current prices, and if long, he puts his stop just below the daily low; if short the stop is placed just above the daily high. If the stop is hit, he is removed from the market, moves to the sidelines, and reevaluates. Fed news is so powerful it can shift the direction of the market for a day, a week, a month, or longer. Therefore, if he is long and there is a new daily low after the news, he wants to be out of the action. There is no need to stay with a trade that is not working. However, because Geof swing trades, he usually has locked in some profits by that time. After he has three up days, he moves his stop/loss order up and reduces risk while locking in profits.

Below is a detailed explanation of one of Geof's recent gold trades when he followed the preceding strategy. In late February 2008, he bought three mini gold futures contracts at $934 an ounce. Following the steps noted earlier, he held those contracts until well into March 2008. He was stopped out of his trade at $999 for a total profit of 65 points per contract. Figure 14.2 graphically depicts the trade and identifies the entry and exit points of this particular gold play.

Geof offers a few words of caution for those wishing to trade gold: If gold drops $50 to $100 in any two-week period, a pullback is coming. Also, if the market gets very quiet and stays in a 10- to 15-point range for a couple

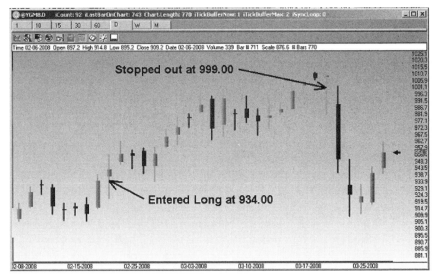

FIGURE 14.2 A daily chart of gold futures. This trade was held for about 20 days.

of weeks and cannot make a new high, expect a correction. If prices drop $40 to $60 an ounce, it is a huge warning and they could go down as much as $140 an ounce.

In the current market, as long as gold is above 772, I will be generally bullish. On October 31, 2007, gold hit a low of 772 following the Fed announcement. Since that date, it has not been below that price.

REVIEW

Gold has been moving up steadily in price since 2003. Gold is an international currency, and traders and investors around the world put cash into gold when they fear the eroding power of inflation will devour their portfolio value. Or, perhaps a major international crisis erupts that may upset financial markets around the world, or traders fear that such an event is imminent. Then they turn to gold as a safe haven where their investment will be more secure than in other markets.

As a rule, I do not day trade gold. However, I often hold gold for the long haul. Geof Smith, our chief instructor at DTI, is an avid gold trader. He frequently trades the shiny metal and uses a swing-trade approach, in which he holds gold for weeks or months. As long as he is making money, he uses a trailing stop, locks in profits, and waits for payday.

As with all investment, respect risk first. Educate yourself about the market and begin slowly. Until gold falls below 772 an ounce, the overall picture is still bullish.

CHAPTER 15

Stocks and ETFs

T he financial markets offer many ways to make money. Some traders master the art of trading stocks, while others concentrate their efforts on futures or bonds. I trade all of these, and much more. In addition to the various products that can be traded, there are also many styles and methods of trading. That is, some traders enjoy day trading, while others see the day trader as a gambler and avoid all associations with that particular trading methodology. Many of these folks tend to be in the market for the long haul. They buy and hold their positions for years and never experiment with any other trading strategy. Then there are swing traders, who fall somewhere in the middle of these two extremes. They buy and hold for days, weeks, or months but do not retain positions for the long term. Money can be made using all of these approaches. However, you need a strategy that works.

People in the industry like to classify everyone. Many people refer to me as exclusively a day trader, but that is not true. Personally, I do not believe in labeling. I think that the market should tell you when to get into and out of a trade. Sometimes that means that you buy and sell in the same session. Other times, that means that you buy this year and sell years from now. If the trade is working and paying you, keep it. If there are no profits or there are losses, consider getting out. Every trading day I look at prices, and generally I trade. In that way, I am a day trader. However, I also hold some positions for weeks or months and I hold others over the long term. I never use a buy, hold, and forget it strategy. Prices change, market conditions shift, and traders and investors must stay abreast of those changes if they want to make money.

FIGURE 15.1 The price movement of IBM and the S&P 500 on May 6, 2008. The chart is a 30-minute chart. The charts follow the same general pattern that is often seen. That is, IBM and the S&P index often mirror each other's movements.

Many volumes have been written about trading stocks, trading mutual funds, and trading exchange-traded funds (ETFs). Here, I want to share just a couple of ideas that might be helpful to you when dealing with these products. First, consider some basic market facts that might help your overall trading performance. Many stocks mirror the movement of the S&P 500 futures or some other futures index. That is, many of the blue chips that are listed on the index will move up or down in close relationship with it. Figure 15.1 shows the parallel movement of the S&P E-mini and IBM on May 6, 2008.

The same fact is also true with other indexes and the big corporations that trade on them. Look at the Nasdaq and Apple on April 6, 2008 (Figure 15.2). The chart on the left is a Nasdaq 30-minute chart of the mini futures index, while the chart on the right is a chart of Apple for the same time frame on the same day. As Figure 15.2 clearly indicates, the images mirror each other.

I maximize my trading hours by trading some of these stocks while I am also trading futures. My StockBox™ software helps me locate stocks to trade. Before trading any stock, I check to be certain that it meets my basic criteria. First, I want the stock price to have a daily average true range (ATR) of at least $1. That is, there must be an average price movement

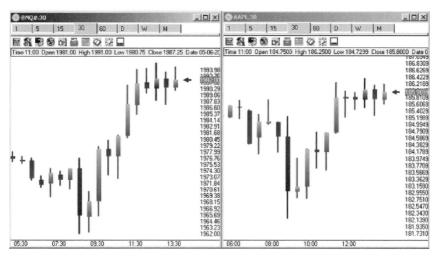

FIGURE 15.2 The movement of prices on the mini Nasdaq and Apple. The movements often mirror each other.

of the equity—either up or down—of at least $1. If the range is too small, there will not be enough room for me to make money. My software does my work for me and prints the numbers on my screen. However, it is possible to determine the ATR of most equities by visiting www.barcharts.com.

Another consideration for short-term stock plays is liquidity. I want to be able to get into my position, and I want to be able to get out of it. Therefore, I must have liquidity. I want a stock with two or three million shares traded during the course of the average business day. That volume will give me enough buyers and sellers to make my play. Again, this information may be obtained from www.barcharts.com.

A vital element of any stock that I trade intraday is beta. Beta is a statistical measure of volatility. It tracks the volatility of a particular equity and gauges that volatility in relation to the overall market. By definition the market has a beta of 1.0. Stocks with a beta less than 1.0 have less volatility than the overall market. Stock with a beta greater than 1.0 are said to have more volatility than the overall market. A stock with a beta of 2.0 is deemed to be twice as volatile as the market. I look for day-trading stocks that have a beta of at least 2.0. Increased volatility may translate into greater danger. That is, prices will generally move farther faster, and if you are on the wrong side of a play, your losses will be greater. However, I want stocks with reasonably high betas because I am looking for a rapid price movement that will pay me. Stocks with low beta move too slowly and are not as appropriate for day trading.

After locating a list of stocks with adequate volume and volatility, I consider the overall market. Is the market bullish or bearish? Then I consider the various sectors. What sectors are moving up? If I go long, I want the overall market to be going my way, and I also want the sector in which the stock is included to also be moving up. The same is true for a short position. I want to move with the current and not fight it.

P E A R L   1 9

When overall market prices have risen 2.5 percent during any session, do not go short.

Finally, I look at the equity indexes. I locate a stock that tends to move in parallel motion with the S&P 500 futures or one of the other indexes, such as the Nasdaq futures. Because I monitor the futures indexes, adding stock trading to my list of strategies is just another way to maximize my use of time and get the most payback for my market knowledge.

As with all trading, I analyze the market and know key numbers before I click the mouse. I never take on a position unless I know not only my entry price but also my profit targets and my stop/loss placement. As with futures contracts, when I get into the market, I simultaneously place orders for profits and stop/loss. Remember to set reasonable profit goals. Rome was not built in a day, and your trading fortune will not be, either.

In addition to intraday stock plays, I also hold some positions for a longer term. Generally, when I hold onto equities, I have some distinct reason for doing so. For example, one stock that I held quite some time was CBOT. The exchanges in general are undergoing a great deal of consolidation and restructuring. Through information in the media, I knew I was holding a product that was escalating in value and would likely continue to do so. Therefore, I let the product and the market tell me when to buy and when to sell. That is the way to make money.

Geof Smith, my friend and coworker, enjoys holding some equities for years. Geof selects his stocks on the basis of his personal knowledge with their products. A few years ago Geof noticed that his wife was writing a lot of checks to Bed Bath & Beyond. Geof researched the company and its product line. He looked at its trading history and liked what he learned. Then he invested in this company. Geof made some money with that particular play and was pleased with his investment. Geof has repeated this process many times over the years. That is, he finds a product he likes. He thinks about the potential for growth for the particular product. Then he investigates the company. Do the numbers look good? If so, he dives in.

The biggest problem that many traders have when trading stocks is that they buy, hold, and forget. Never do that. There are too many variables in the market that can cause your stocks to fall in price. If you are not watching the price action, before you know it you have lost 20 percent, 40 percent, or more of your value. Even though the market may again rise to pre-sell-off prices, it may take months or years. Instead of riding the investment down, you could have liquidated the particular investment and moved those funds into another area, where the value could have been preserved or grown.

PEARL 20

Like your stock choices, but do not marry them. When they stop paying, it is time to split.

Another good thing to remember is that stocks are generally selected because you like the company or the product. Like your choices, but do not marry them. Stay with the stock as long as it pays, but when the fun is over, move on. At the altar it may be "until death do us part," but on Wall Street it is just "until the money stops coming into the bank." If the stock is not paying you, get rid of it. Any time that a stock drops 10 percent, I begin considering my exit strategy. If the overall market goes up by 2 percent in a session while your stock moves down in price—get out.

PEARL 21

If the general market is moving up and your stock is not, you have a problem. Specifically, if the overall market moves up by 2 percent and your stock is moving down—get out!

It may seem contrary to logic, but often the stocks that have been the most bullish in an up-market will fall the fastest in a downturn. That is one of the reasons that it is hard for investors and traders to liquidate positions. After all, these have been the shares that have been strongly moving up and adding valuation to the portfolio. It is hard to let them go.

PEARL 22

Stocks that have been the most bullish typically fall the fastest in a downtrending market.

THE WAVE OF THE FUTURE—ETFs

Another way to trade stocks is to trade mutual funds or use ETFs. ETFs are not new. They have been around since the late 1980s and early 1990s. However, in recent years, they have gained much popularity. ETFs are traded on stock exchanges just like any equity. However, when you buy an ETF, you are buying a group of investments. In this way they are somewhat similar to a mutual fund. Most ETFs are index funds. For example, the Spyder is an ETF for S&P 500 stocks. The QQQQ is a similar fund holding a Nasdaq portfolio. The Diamond is the same, but for the Dow Jones 30. These ETFs are traded on the American Exchange. In addition to the well-known and popular ETFs, there are many others. I regularly trade OIH, which is an oil-based ETF.

Trading ETFs offers a number of advantages. First, they are less news sensitive. If your portfolio is heavy with one particular stock and that corporation has lower-than-expected earnings or their product is defective and faces a recall, or any number of other bad events befall the corporation, your portfolio is devastated. With the ETF, the stock is just one of many, and the effects of a corporation-specific problem are minimized.

By definition, an ETF offers a level of diversity. With an ETF you acquire an interest in a basket of financial products. However, ETFs differ from mutual funds in that shares may be bought and sold intraday like stocks. Many ETFs may be electronically traded.

I regularly trade ETFs. In this oil boom, OIH has grabbed my attention. I use the same strategies to trade ETFs that I use for stocks. That is, I check liquidity, volume, and beta. In the current market, the OIH fund had been a great one for me to trade, and at the time of this writing, I trade it several times each week. If you are unfamiliar with ETFs, I suggest you begin educating yourself. These are great profit centers. In fact, I predict that in the not-too-distant future, mutual funds will be out of favor and everyone will be trading ETFs instead. They simply offer too many advantages to be missed.

REVIEW

The financial markets offer a wide array of products. During the course of any day, week, month, or year, there is much that can be traded. Stocks may be traded intraday, for the long term, or somewhere in between. The main thing to remember is that you do not want to keep a stock that is not paying you. Once the profits fall, get out of that particular play.

I spend a great deal of time watching the markets, especially the equity index futures, such as the S&P 500 and the Dow and Nasdaq futures. One of the ways that I take advantage of this knowledge and information is by trading stocks that tend to move in unison with one of the indexes. In that way I am getting paid from two profit centers, the index and the stock.

When I trade stocks intraday, I look for shares that have a good average trading range. I want the stock to move at least $1 in price during the average session. If it does not do so, I will not trade it because it will not offer me the possibility to make money. Also, I want a stock that has good volume so that I can find a buyer for my shares when I want to liquidate them. I am looking for a stock with two to three million shares trading every day. Volatility is another important factor. I am looking for a beta around 2.0. When all of these criteria are met, I look at the market. When going long, I want the sector of which the stock is a part to be going in my direction. I also want the overall market to be supporting my play.

In addition to trading stocks, I also trade ETFs. I trade them like stocks because in many ways they act like equities and are traded like them. ETFs are the wave of the future. They offer many advantages and allow traders the diversity of a mutual fund as well as the flexibility and liquidity of stocks.

PART THREE

The
Wild Cards

CHAPTER 16

Beyond the
Numbers

I n the basic trading class at DTI, we explain that the DTI trading method is like a three-legged stool. Each of the legs is needed if the stool is going to function properly. If one leg is absent, the stool will collapse. Trading resembles the stool in that it, too, has three important parts to its foundation: time, key numbers, and market indicators. Without each of these fundamental elements, you will not be a good trader. You will not be able to read the market's tape correctly and consistently make winning plays. Like the stool, without all three legs, your trading will not have stability and you will not achieve success. Yet, effective trading requires far more than mastering these three basic quantifiable skills. It requires an array of other talents and abilities including discipline, impartiality, persistence, attitude, and commitment. In addition, trading involves a great deal of psychology. I will discuss that in a later chapter. Here, I want to talk about some of the attributes of effective traders. These are the intangible elements of trading that are so powerful in determining the success or failure of a trader.

WINNERS TRADE THE NUMBERS

Sometimes I stand in front of the classroom and ask my students, "Is the market going up or down today? Do you want to go long or short?" I generally see a hand shoot up and one student boldly answers the question. "The markets are bullish, and I think we're going up." On any given day that might be correct. Then again, it might just as well be incorrect. The truth is that no one knows how the markets will trade. No one has a crystal ball to gaze into the future. Sometimes prices move irrationally. In spite of economic factors, there are times when prices take on a life of their own and move in an illogical manner. Sometimes there seems to be neither rhyme nor reason to the price action. It is unpredictable and surprising. Therefore, keep an open mind and let the market tell you whether to be long, short, or out.

Most traders have a bias. We look at the markets every day, and we focus on the prices and the economic conditions that surround them. It is only natural that we would have an opinion about the market's sentiment and direction. Having a bias is not a problem. Trading on the basis of bias is a problem. Bias blinds you from focusing on the numbers. It gives you a preconceived view of the market and causes you to make bad trades that are not supported by the data.

I explained in Chapter 8 my strategy for trading the Fed rate announcements. Those announcements are scheduled eight times a year. If you watch prices just before the news is released, you will see prices jumping. Traders cannot wait to place their trades. They feel so certain that they know not only what action the Fed is taking but also the market's response to that action that they cannot keep their hand off the computer mouse. They have a market bias, and they are putting their money at risk on the basis of that bias. If you ever watch me trade the Fed, you will see that I do not place a trade until the news is out and the market has shown me the direction. I do not hope or guess; I watch prices, read the tape, and follow the market's lead. Using that strategy, I am able to make money.

Each day when you approach the markets, you may have an opinion as to where they will go during the session. However, keep that opinion in perspective and do not allow it to cloud your reasoning or affect your judgment. Never trade on the basis of bias. Let the numbers and the indicators show the way. Then follow. There is no problem with having a bias as long as you do not rely on that bias for trading. In other words, have an opinion, but do not trade on that alone. Have market confirmation for any trade.

BE DISCIPLINED

Electronic exchanges, computerized trading platforms, real-time data feed—all of these innovations make trading easy. In fact, it is almost too easy. Just click the mouse and play the game. Overtrading is the biggest problem of most day traders. Because they spend most of their days sitting in front of a computer screen, they feel compelled to trade. When they are not trading, they feel that they are not doing their job. Therefore, they manufacture trades and see trade setups everywhere. Every time a trade is made, money is at risk. Therefore, it makes no sense to trade unless the odds of success favor a win.

Over the years, I have seen many people who were very intelligent and had most of the skills they needed to become really good traders. But they lacked discipline. They made so many trades every day that they left my head spinning. To gain discipline, establish some rules. Set aside specific times during the day when you will trade. Outside of those times, close the trading platform or at least walk away from the computer. In addition to establishing some designated trading times throughout the day, also hold yourself to some trading standards. Do not take just any trade. Use the "T" Square approach and use good analysis. Be discriminating. After all, it is your money that is on the line. Each day brings many possible trades. Take only the good ones that are timely and supported by key numbers and market indicators.

KISS YOUR EGO GOODBYE

No one is perfect, and no trader always makes winning trades. Even the pros lose money some of the time. However, when the pros are on the losing side, they manage their money. That is, they admit defeat, exit the trade, and move to the sidelines. The pros do not enjoy losing, but they accept it gracefully. Egomaniacs do not manage their money because they stay with losers too long. They simply cannot admit that they are wrong and liquidate the position. Losing money is painful but it is simply a part of trading. Some trades are losers. In fact, some weeks and months are losers. I encourage traders to put their losing trades in the proper perspective. As a trader, remember that any single trade is just one trade among many. There will be dozens, hundreds, perhaps thousands of other trades. If you preserve your capital, you can stay in the game for the long haul. In that context, a losing trade is nothing to cry about. Learn from it and move on.

BE PERSISTENT

Benjamin Franklin is credited with saying that energy and persistence conquer all things. Calvin Coolidge, the thirtieth president of the United States, did not go that far, but he, too, believed that persistence was one of the most important aspects of success. Coolidge said, "Nothing in the world can take the place of Persistence. Talent will not; nothing is more common than unsuccessful men with talent. Genius will not; unrewarded genius is almost a proverb. Education will not, the world is full of educated derelicts. Persistence and determination alone are omnipotent. The slogan 'Press On' has solved and will solve the problems of the human race." Those who quit will never experience success. That is a fact of life and of trading.

Trading is difficult. There are many skills to master. In addition to analyzing the markets and reading the tape successfully, you must learn to operate the trading platform correctly, be disciplined, and stay balanced. You must also preserve your capital and manage risk. Faced with such daunting challenges, many would-be traders quit. They do not have the persistence to become winners.

If you want to learn to be a trader, you must stay in the game long enough to master it. Do not be too easily defeated. When you lose, do not be destroyed by it. Become more determined to do better. Put the loss in the proper perspective and move on.

PATIENCE PAYS

I love to trade. Trading is fun. Electronic trading platforms resemble video games, and all it takes to get into the action is just a click of the computer mouse. However, such careless trading will lead to disaster. Never trade for sport. Trade to make money. That means that most of the day should be spent in analysis and evaluation. Only when good opportunities are present should you get into the market. It takes a great deal of patience to watch prices move and stay out of the action.

However, staying out is a market position and a good one. There are three actions that a trader may take: he can be long, short, or out of the market. Winners opt to be out of the market most of the time. They realize that the smart approach to trading is to trade only when the odds of success are good. If market conditions are not ideal, they do not trade.

One of the simplest steps that many traders can take to make more money and gain trading consistency is to stop trading at the drop of a dime and have the patience to wait for the right trade.

BELIEVE IN YOURSELF

Even on a good day, trading is hard. There is much to gauge, measure, and evaluate. Faced with such a daunting challenge, it is easy to become discouraged and lose confidence in your abilities. In trading, like many other areas of life, having a winning attitude is critical. I have heard it said that the market pays you what you think you are worth. If you do not respect your abilities, neither will Wall Street. Evaluate each trade carefully and follow the rules; if the odds for success are in your favor, have the confidence to take the trade and expect it to pay you. If you do not believe the trade is going to work, do not take it. Sit on the sidelines and wait for a better setup that meets all of the criteria of a winner. The markets will be here tomorrow. If you do not feel good about any trades today, stay out of the market and wait until the numbers and the indicators strongly support your play.

REVIEW

Trading is not easy. It requires the mastery of many different skills and abilities. If making money on Wall Street required only the ability to read the tape, many intelligent and educated people could do it. However, trading takes more than quantifiable information. Trading decisions get clouded by bias, ego, and lack of patience and many other attributes that traders are lacking. It is those "soft" skills like patience and good judgment that make trading an art and not a science. Furthermore, it is those skills that make good traders.

CHAPTER 17

Risk
Management

G ood risk management is critical to any trading strategy. A bit of advice that the experts always give is to cut losses quickly but let winners run. That sounds simple, but it is one of the most difficult aspects of trading. I have heard it said that if the right risk management techniques are used, it is possible to make money with almost any strategy. I do not believe that is true, but I certainly believe that without risk management, any strategy is doomed to fail.

Every trader will make losing trades. Professionals make them all the time. However, when a professional makes a bad trade, he knows how to limit the amount of money he loses. An amateur will hold a losing position and allow his trading account to be bled dry. For that reason, I have several techniques that I recommend to my students and that I use myself. By using these techniques on a regular basis, you are able to hold losses to reasonable limits.

The first step to managing risk in general is to determine your personal risk tolerance. Some folks have more money than others. They may be able to lose $100,000 and not feel much pain. However, another trader may feel extreme pain when he loses a few thousand dollars. A friend of mine recently explained to me his strategy for trading precious metals. I asked about stop/loss placement for his trades. Frankly, the amount of risk seemed a little high to me and I asked about it. "Isn't that too much risk to take?" He leaned back in his chair and smiled, "Not for me." I understood the message. He was financially resourced enough to bear that risk without working up a sweat. Furthermore, his strategy was a good one and it was consistently paying him. Traders with less cash should not be using his strategy unless they can afford to take the same level of risk that he is able to comfortably take. Never take a trade if the risk is too great for you and your financial situation. Always determine how much you can afford to lose. If you will suffer dire consequences if the trade is a bad one or if you will lose a lot of sleep worrying about the trade—do not take it. No one likes to lose money, and we all get angry when the market takes anything from us. However, there is a big difference between losing some spare cash and losing the rent money or the mortgage payment. I firmly believe that if risk is considered first, the rewards will come. Never enter a trade until you know the risk involved and are able and willing to take those risks. I teach my students a number of strategies to help them preserve capital.

THREE STRIKES AND YOU ARE OUT

On the ball field, a batter gets three strikes and then the umpire calls him out. Whether he likes it or not, that batter is leaving the field for the dugout. He is no longer standing at home plate swinging a bat. Even though there is no umpire standing beside you as you trade, you need to call yourself out after three strikes. In other words, if you take three trades in a row and all three are losers—STOP. Something is wrong. Your analysis is faulty and you are not reading the tape correctly. Or the market is not responding as usual. Maybe some external factor is altering prices or something else is happening. The reason really does not matter. The important fact is that you are off your game. Sometimes it is possible to manage losses well and not lose a great deal of money, but that is not the issue. Regardless of the amount of monetary loss, if you have made three bad trades in a row, close the trading platform and do something else. It is not your day to trade.

Some traders apply this rule to their weekly trading. If during the course of any given week they make three bad trades, they stop. When the strategy is not working or the execution of the strategy is faulty, continuing to trade will merely pile up losses and deplete the trading account. As the old adage goes, "Stop while you are ahead"—or at least before you are too far in the hole.

LIMIT RISK

I hold my losses down by never risking more than a small percentage of my overall portfolio on any trade. If possible, risk only a small percentage of the account balance on any trade. In that way, if you make several bad trades, you will not deplete the trading account. Remember that when the account is empty, you are out of the trading game.

Another way to keep losses low is to never risk more than one-third of the average true range (ATR) of a product on any single trade. At the time of this writing, the ATR of the E-mini S&P is about 20 points. Therefore, in this market I will not risk more than 6 or 7 points on any trade. In fact, I generally risk about half that amount. I know that if I keep losses low, I can recoup them on future trades. If you allow a few trades to take you to the cleaners, it is too hard to make back that cash. Money that you do not lose today is money that you do not have to make tomorrow.

One problem all traders have is that we all hate to lose. Therefore, there is a tendency to hold trades and hope for a reversal. Dreaming and hoping will not make you money. The only way to make money is to be on the right side of the action. Therefore, if a trade is not paying, admit that a mistake has been made and get out while the loss is small. Hoping and dreaming have no place in trading.

USE THE TWO-MINUTE RULE

When I am day trading, I want to be paid on some portion of my position in two minutes. I know that fact sounds unrealistic to many of my readers, but that is how most of my day-trading strategies work. I carefully select my trading times and wait for a price move in my favor. If that move does not happen quickly, I am probably wrong. I made a mistake. It is not the end of the world. I just exit the position and wait for a better opportunity when my analysis is more on the money.

Since my day-trading strategies work quickly, I suggest to my students that they check the clock when they enter a trade. In fact, I have a clock built into my RoadMap™ software for this purpose. DTI students can click on the clock and time the trade. If the two minutes expire and they are not making money, they need to reevaluate the trade. Are the indicators and key numbers still on their side? If so, they may hang with the trade a little longer. If not, it is probably time to exit and move to the sideline. Prices can move against a position quickly, and if an error has been made, there is no need to let it eat up your cash. Take the loss and forget it.

USE STOP/LOSS ORDERS

One of the easiest steps that you can take to limit losses is to use a stop/loss order. Before entering the trade you must identify the price point at which the market will prove you wrong. For example, if you are going long, where is support? If support is broken to the downside, the market is probably heading down to the next tier of support. Why hold on at that point? Get out. Or, if you are short, where is resistance? If resistance is broken, the bulls are stronger than you thought. That means the market is telling you that you are wrong. Listen to the message. Before taking a trade, identify those points and put a stop/loss order there. In that way the market will take you out and your financial loss will be limited.

Once you are in a trade, the desire to win becomes very strong, sometimes overwhelming. Even when a stop/loss order is used, traders will sometimes move it to stay with the trade longer and give the market more room to move. As prices move against the trade and toward the stop/loss order, these undisciplined traders just move the stop and keep losing money. Once the stop/loss order is placed, *never* move it farther from the trading price. In some conditions you may want to move it closer, but never farther away. If the trade is not working, there is no reason to give the market more of your cash. If a loss is going to be suffered, better to take it sooner than later. In that way the loss will be less.

PEARL 23

Take losses more quickly than profits.

I suggest that traders use stop/loss orders with every trade. A stop is not guaranteed to work under all market conditions. In the stock market, prices may gap down. For example, if you are short a blue-chip stock and the company announces earning after the exchange on which it is traded has closed, prices may gap up at the next day's open. You will not get your hoped-for stop/loss price. That is, there may be slippage. But there is some protection with a stop/loss, even under these conditions. Also, in a crash, the stop/loss price may not be hit. Prices may surge past it. Nevertheless, you should always use a stop. In orderly market conditions, stop/loss orders will work as planned and offer protection.

PEARL 24

Always use a stop.

HAVE AN EXIT STRATEGY

Never take a trade unless you know where you will get out of it. There are two price points that you should know when you click that mouse.

First, establish profit targets. Where do you expect to exit the trade with money in your pocket? Be realistic in setting this goal. There is a popular show on television that fascinates me. It is called *Deal or No Deal*. In the show, contestants play the odds and try to win a million dollars. Most of the contestants have no idea of how to calculate the odds. All they think about is that they came hoping to win a million. Even when there is no longer any hope that they will succeed, they keep risking everything to keep trying. Even when the odds are hugely against them, they will keep playing the game and hoping for that elusive million. The smart contestants work their way up to a nice sum—maybe even a few hundred thousand dollars—take the money, and go home. They understand that what you want and what you get are not always the same. You have to be realistic in establishing your goals.

Trading, like *Deal or No Deal*, is all about the odds. Just like the contestants on the show, when you get into a trade, you want to make a lot of money from it. But you have to be reasonable. How much profit can you realistically expect from the trade in light of the time of day and the key numbers near your entry price? If the ATR of the S&P 500 E-mini futures is 18 points during the course of the session and it has already moved 15 of those points, do not expect to make 20 points of profit. It is possible that you could do that, but the odds of doing so are not in your favor. Therefore, look at the market and the key numbers and determine profit targets. Set the first profit target at the first key number that you hit. For example, if you are short, take at least some profits at the nearest level of support. If you are long, take at least some portion of your positions off at the next level of resistance. If the market is strong enough, there might be a move through and above resistance or through and below support. In that case, a second profit target could be placed at that resistance or support level. The important thing to remember is that when a trade is made, know where profit will be taken. Do not settle for pennies when dollars can be made. Consistently doing this will cause you to lose money. The reason is simple: you will have losses. You need money to offset them and to add value to your account. If you take big losses and little profits, you are going broke. Do not be greedy, but remember not to sell yourself and the market short.

PEARL 25

When you hear someone say, "You do not go broke taking profits," RUN. That is exactly how it happens.

When the mouse is clicked and the trade is entered, follow through immediately with profit orders. Get them in the market, not just in your head. In that way, when prices reach your target, your orders will be in line for execution. Limit orders are generally used for profit taking. With limit orders, you are not guaranteed a fill. The orders are filled on a first-come, first-served basis. If there are 3000 orders waiting to be filled at $1400 and you are order 3001, you may not get filled and prices may move against you. Get in the cue early by executing your profit orders immediately after you take on your position.

PEARL 26

When entering a position, always know where the exit resides.

In addition to profit targets, always know where you will place your stop/loss order. Many traders use mental stops. Those do not work well. Often, we plan to get the stop/loss orders in and just do not do so. Instead, prices move against our position and we just keep holding the position and losing more and more money. If the stop/loss order is placed at the same time that the trade is made, it helps keep us honest and real.

MANAGE EVERY TRADE

Over the years, I have learned the importance of managing every trade that I make. I have losing trades and I lose money—every trader does. But I am a hands-on trader and when I see prices going against me, I react. When a trade is not going my way, I may tighten my stop and move it closer to the trading price, or I may liquidate some of my positions without making a profit or with a small loss. I will not hold all of my positions and sit on my thumbs while the market takes me to the cleaners.

Once in a trade, I keep my eyes on key numbers and market indicators. If market indicators like the NYSE tick, the Nasdaq tick, or the V-Factor turn against my position, I react. If a key number is broken in an unpredictable manner, I respond. In the old days, I used a different strategy. If prices moved against my position, I added to the position. For example, if I took a long position in IBM and IBM fell in price, I added to the position at the lower price. If prices continued to deteriorate, I continued to buy until I had invested my entire amount of cash. Many traders use that approach today. It is called averaging down. Today, I know the foolishness of such a strategy and do not do it. Why fight the market? If prices are going down, I will not be a buyer. I will liquidate my long position before too much money is lost.

PEARL 27

Never risk too much with any trade. No trade is worth losing more than 10 percent of your account balance.

Electronic trading platforms offer many advantages over phoning orders to a broker. With electronic exchanges a trade can be quickly executed, and in seconds, or split seconds, it is possible to know if the order was filled and at what price. By trading electronically, you are able to have much greater control over many aspects of the trade. However, there are some drawbacks to the new technology. It is easy to become separated from your money. Suddenly, the cash in the trading account does not feel real. It is just a group of numbers at the bottom of a trading platform. So what if $500 or $1000 are lost today? You can make up all of that money and more tomorrow. Then, day after day, the losses mount and the account balance drops. Reality finally hits home when a margin call comes from the broker. Never become separated from your money! Every dollar that is lost is important. Make wise decisions and be sure the odds are on your side before you click that mouse and make any trading decision.

PHASING INTO AND OUT OF POSITIONS

Another way to manage risk is to phase into and out of positions. I do this with all of my trades. I trade in multiples of three. That is, I generally buy 3, 6, 9, 30, and so on, contracts. In that way I am able to take profit at various levels and reduce the risk associated with the trade. If I have six contracts, I will liquidate two of them with a few ticks of profit. That action puts a little cash into my account and reduces my exposure. As the market moves in my favor, I liquidate another two contracts with more profit. Now my profits from the trade are increasing and my risk is decreasing. I have only two contracts at risk in the market, and I have already made money to cover the potential loss that I may suffer on those contracts. I move my stop/loss up to a breakeven level. Now I am trading with the market's money. I have taken enough money out of the market to pay for my trade. This is an ideal position to be in because I can liquidate the position whenever I want and not lose a penny. I can take profits or hold them to follow a longer trend. I am in the driver's seat and I can hold 'em or fold 'em when I choose.

Years ago, I used an all-or-nothing strategy. I was greedy and tried to ride all of my positions for maximum profits. I took an all-or-nothing approach, and many times I got nothing. Now I moderate my greed and take profits at various profit levels. I do not want to give the market the opportunity to turn a winning trade into a loser. By using the approach outlined above, even if my ultimate profit target is never reached, I am generally able to walk away with some profits. Also, even on my bad trades, I am able to reduce my loss.

Another way that this strategy can be used is to phase into positions. For example, maybe you feel reasonably comfortable about taking a position but want to move forward with caution. Take a small position as a probe. If the trade works and is confirmed by a move in your favor, add to the position. For example, if you take a probe to the long side and a big resistance number is broken to the upside, add to the position and ride it up to the next point of resistance. Be sure to use stop/loss orders and watch the trade carefully.

DIVERSIFY

One of the safest ways to control risk with your overall portfolio is to diversify. Don't put all of your eggs in one basket. When the technology stocks took a beating in 2000, many people suffered huge losses because the bulk of their investments were in that sector. Profits had been so strong that they ignored the basic principles of diversification and put everything into the high-tech sector. When the Nasdaq dropped, their portfolios were slashed. The Nasdaq has still not even recovered to the 50 percent level of those highs seen prior to the crash. Do not put your long-term stock portfolio in only one sector. Even if profits are good, the picture may change and you need to be prepared.

In addition to diversifying the portfolio among sectors, diversify among different types of assets. Balance the portfolio with bonds, real estate, and perhaps even commodities and precious metals. If stocks go down, gold should go up. In the current market, oil is strong and getting stronger as time passes. The more diversification you have, the more resistance you have to market conditions.

REVIEW

No market strategy can succeed without good risk management. As a trader, you must respect risk and preserve your trading capital. When you get into a trade, know where you will take profits and where you will get out if prices move against you. Do not use mental stops—it is too easy to become mesmerized by prices and lose too much money. If the stop/loss order is placed when the order is executed, it will save you money.

Be a hands-on trader. Watch every trade, and if you have made a mistake and the trade goes against you—get out. Do not hold losers and allow them to deplete your cash. When you have a winner, let a portion of the position run while you follow the move with a trailing stop. Lock in profits and enjoy taking as much money from the market as the trade will allow.

All traders go through tough times. Sometimes a strategy is not working. The market conditions are wrong or unpredictable. Or perhaps your execution is not right. At any rate, there are times when you are simply not playing a good game. After several losses in a row, stop trading and move to the sidelines. Analyze and observe. Only after a break should you try again. Then begin slowly and regain confidence and confirm skills.

CHAPTER 18

Psychology and Discipline: The Winner's Edge

I n 1989, Stephen Covey wrote his mega-seller, *The Seven Habits of Highly Effective People* (Free Press, 1989). Since that time, Covey has gained the respect of leaders and managers from all walks of life. Through his books and his institute, he has taught thousands of people how to become more effective in managing and living both their business and personal lives. Reading about the seven habits will probably not have a lasting impact on anyone. However, taking action and using the seven habits will make a difference. One of my friends, Mike Dow, was the mayor of Mobile, Alabama, for 16 years. Shortly after being elected, he attended one of Covey's courses. When he came home from the institute, he worked diligently to put the principles that he had learned into practice. Mike says that the information he learned from that course changed his life. Mike is known throughout the community as a man who gets things done. He did not learn a theory or read about some ideas and put them on a shelf. He put the ideas into practice and he got results. The more he practiced the seven habits, the more ingrained they became in his routine. After all of these years, I think he is a walking example of those principles. Mike put the principles into practice. He disciplined himself to carry out the principles and rules that he had learned.

As with the seven habits, it will do you no good to read trading strategies if you do not exercise control and execute them correctly. To be a good trader you must have discipline and control. Over the years, I have seen many people aspire to become professional traders. They learn winning strategies. However, they either cannot or will not stick to the rules and carry out the strategies effectively. They make dozens of trades every day and do not manage their money. They pay the price and are soon out of the market for good.

Trading is fun. The trading dome resembles a video game and prices move up and down continuously. Being in a trade is exciting. In addition to the fun of the game, if the trade works, you will even get paid for having so much entertainment. Many traders forget that the purpose of trading is to make money. They begin playing for sport or for amusement. They want to be in a trade all the time. Consequently, they are soon not trading at all because they are broke.

The biggest problem with electronic trading is overtrading. It is too easy to click the mouse and jump into the market. However, if the trade was not analyzed and planned, it may be a little harder to get out of—at least with a profit. Day traders often feel compelled to trade all day long. After all, that is their job. If they look at the computer screen, they must find a trade somewhere or they are not working. The problem is that far too many of those trades should never have been taken, and the thoughtless trader loses his shirt.

PEARL 28

Overtrading makes you lose—don't lose.

Many traders do not realize that being out of the market is a position. When there is no winning opportunity, the "out" position is the wisest one to make. Never trade unless the odds of success are on your side. Keep your money in your account and let those who are foolish enough to chase after losing trades throw their account away. It is far better to miss some trades than to overtrade. Remember that the market will be there tomorrow. If you let a few good trades go, it is okay. Look for the right setup during the next session and be ready to take the trade. Stay disciplined and keep the odds in your favor. Without discipline, you will not be a good trader. In fact, without discipline, you will not be a trader at all.

THE PSYCHOLOGY OF WINNING

In addition to all of the other variables associated with trading, there is one more wild card that is so powerful it can torpedo even the best trade: emotion. Few endeavors are more emotionally charged than trading. Money is precious to most of us, and when we face the possibility that we may lose it, we experience emotional turmoil that we have never experienced before. A few of the overpowering feelings with which we must deal are fear, greed, arrogance, shame, glee, and panic. These emotions may be so powerful that we act in ways we did not anticipate and our behavior becomes self-destructive and financially harmful.

Greed Is Deadly

We are traders because we enjoy making money. The more money we make, the more satisfaction we obtain from the pursuit. Translation: we are all greedy. We want to make the most money we can on every trade. We hate leaving money on the table, and we do not want to lose a dime. Greed, when it is uncontrolled, will lead us to take risky trades and to stay with losing trades too long. Once greed gains the upper hand, we begin looking for more and more chances to make money. The result is that our analysis becomes faulty and we dismiss warning signals. A trader who is searching for a trade might say to himself, "The NYSE issues are still weak, but the futures indexes are moving up. If I buy now, I can get a jump on the market and make more money." Or "I need to short something and I need to do it NOW. The S&P 500 is heading down." In your haste to get the green, you may forget to note that the S&P is trading at a strong support level and the Nasdaq and Dow futures are not looking nearly as bleak as the S&P that you just shorted. The result of such hasty actions will be loss and eventually the consequences may be your total destruction as a trader. The only way to succeed in trading is to recognize and moderate greed so that it does not sabotage your trading.

In addition to getting you into losing trades, greed will also be responsible for holding trades too long—both winners and loser. You will hold winners because you do not want to leave a penny on the table. You are never satisfied with the profits you have and want more. When holding winners too long, they often turn to loser. Therefore, take reasonable profits and be happy. You will not get rich on every trade. It is the process of consistently making good trades and earning money that may get you riches. When you enter a trade you should know where support and resistance are located. If you are long and prices near a resistance point, take some profits on all or a portion of your trades. Do not take an all-or-nothing approach. Put some money in the bank. Far too often, those traders who want all or nothing get nothing.

Greed can also add to losses. It is hard to admit a mistake. Years ago, I liked to fool myself. I would tell myself that a loss was not a loss unless and until I liquidated the position. As long as I was in the trade, there was a chance that the market would go my way. I would hold on because I did not think I could take the loss. I was just too greedy to accept it gracefully. Hoping that the market will pay you is an ineffective trading strategy. Read the tape, and if the trade is a loser, don't hold on. Let it go. Accept the loss and be happy that you have monitored the trade and alleviated the loss.

Fear Is Lethal

The flip side of greed is fear. We all fear making mistakes and bad trades. Losing money is painful. It hurts the bank account and it damages our egos. Everyone enjoys bragging about winning trades, but we all hate to think about the losers. Like greed, fear can be a trader's worst enemy. If not tamed, it will lead to paralysis. Good trades will come and go without an entry. While we are doing one final analysis or checking just one more indicator, the opportunity will be lost and so will the chance to make money. Or if we manage to garner enough courage to click the mouse and execute a trade, we are too afraid to let the trade work. If there is even a hint of a problem, we grab the mouse and liquidate the position with a loss. Fear is a formidable foe.

Do not act with haste when trading. Have a tested strategy. Know how to properly execute that strategy. Then when the set up is present, have the courage to click the mouse and take the trade. You cannot make money in the markets if you are always sitting on the sidelines.

Another problem with fear is that it prevents you from maximizing the moneymaking opportunity in a trade. Prices always bobble up and down. Fearful traders get anxious if the market even hints that the trade may be a loser. One bobble against them and they hit the panic button and liquidate the position. They either exit with little to no profit or with a loss. Often, they do not give the trade time to work. Even when all indicators are confirming the move, they assume they have been wrong. Fearful traders will not make money on Wall Street. It takes confidence to make money.

Other Toxic Emotions

An emotion that is closely associated with fear is humility. Some traders just do not have enough faith and confidence in themselves. Even when the indicators justify a buy, they sit and wait for a perfect set up. If every index and every indicator is yelling to sell, they question their ability to analyze and execute the trade correctly. While they are waiting to have the conviction to trade, the market moves on without them.

Then there are the "perfect" traders. They know it all. They never make mistakes—at least not any that they acknowledge. Their trading lives are short-lived because their arrogance takes them out of the game quickly. Everyone makes mistakes. Even professional traders make a lot of mistakes. The difference between the pros and the arrogant amateur is that the professional knows that he will make errors and is prepared to accept and respond appropriately to them. The pros use good risk management to limit losses and keep them in proper perspective.

There are several ways that I balance these destructive emotions and keep my trading on track. First, I recognize the problem and face it. Knowing the risk of a trade before I take it helps me reduce fear. To determine my risk I identify the price point where the market will prove me wrong. That is my maximum exposure. If the price moves to that point, I no longer want to be in the trade because the odds of success are not in my favor. Knowing the risk calms my fears. If I am unwilling or unable to take the risk, I do not take the trade.

For example, if the S&P 500 futures open at $1331 and begin selling off. I might take a short position. As long as prices stay below the open and continue downward, I'm okay. But if the bulls start buying and prices move up strongly and cross into positive territory above the opening price, I have to reevaluate my trade. Perhaps I have made a mistake and it is time to bail. An important resistance number has been broken and the market is sending me a message. Identifying the risk before clicking the mouse tames my fears and allows me to focus on the numbers and the trade rather than my emotions.

Another essential step to reducing fear is preparation. Before I trade, I am ready. I have identified key numbers. I know the indicators I will watch. I have identified the times when I will look to trade and the times I will sit on the sidelines. When the session begins, I know the buying and selling areas that I am anticipating. If the market goes there, I am ready to make my move. Being prepared reduces fear.

In addition to the normal fears that all traders face, novice traders are also fearful that they cannot operate the equipment correctly or handle the trading platform. These are real fears and they must be dealt with. I'm from the deep south, and I do not have the chance to go skiing very often. However, occasionally I dare to hit the slopes. When I first started skiing, I had to adjust to the sensation of gliding downhill. Standing on top of a mountain and looking at the bottom of the ski run can be a sobering sight. What if my speed is too great and I am heading for a tree? Or a person? Can I stop? Do I have the skills to safely make my way down the slope? It is a real fear. However, once I mastered the art of control, my fears diminished. When I knew I could stop when I needed to do so, I was no longer afraid to point my skis downward and lean into the move. Only then was I able to be carefree and enjoy the fun of skiing. I was in charge and fear was held in check.

For the novice, trading is like standing atop a mountain and fearing that you have no control when skiing down it. What if there is a need to stop? What if you head for a tree or a dropoff? Will you be able to stop on the slope and prevent injury? In trading the question is: Can you get out of the trade quickly enough if prices move against the play? Traders who do not have experience executing the trading platform are often very fearful, and rightly so. The solution to this particular problem is experience and practice. Most brokers offer the opportunity to execute simulations. If you are a beginner, do them and do a lot of them. By using the simulation platform you are able to learn how to get into and out of positions with ease. You are also able to experience the consequences of placing the wrong type of order. All beginners have inadvertently executed a market order when a stop order was the aim. Or they have executed a stop order when a limit order was the preference. Only through experience can these problems be avoided. Even very experienced traders make mistakes with order types from time to time. Practice will keep this particular error to a minimum. Once you develop the skills to move in and out of the market quickly and on your terms, there is far less fear with electronic trading.

Unless traders understand the role that emotions play in making decisions and executing trades, they are doomed to fail.

GAINING BALANCE

One of the most important steps that I take to conquer fear and greed is to balance the risk. By phasing out of positions at various profit levels, I am able to relinquish some contracts to fear while holding others to satisfy greed. I do this by trading multiple contracts or shares. I like to trade in multiples of three. That is, I buy three S&P 500 contracts, or 15, or 30, depending on the play and my faith in it. In that way, I am able to exit portions of my positions at various prices. That allows me to take some profits early and reduce my risk and my fear. I am also able to hold some positions to appease greed by riding a trend to greater profits. I call this strategy the "Three T's of Trading."

Assume I am buying the E-mini S&P 500 at $1335.75. Market conditions favor my play, and I buy 15 e-mini contracts. Through observation and analysis of key numbers, I know that some resistance will likely step into the market at $1337 and additional resistance at 1339. However, I anticipate a move to the $1342 area or higher based on the strength of the market. Therefore, I want to take some of my positions off the table quickly. I take a few ticks of profit on one-third of my positions at $1336.50. With three ticks of profit or $37.50 per contract, I am able to gross $187.50 on the lot. I refer to this part of the trade as the "Tick." Now my risk is reduced, as I am holding only 10 contracts. I liquidate another five contracts at $1338.75.

I make three points on the play, or $150 per contract. I now add that $450 to the $187.50 I have already earned. This is what I refer to as the "Trade" portion of the maneuver. With $637.50 in the bank, I am far less fearful of the trade. I am now holding only five contracts. I can move my stop to $1335 and my total exposure is only $187.50. Or I can place my stop at my entry point and use the market's money to finish the trade. Now my risk is small and my fear is tamed. Now I am in total control and fearless. I can take my profits and exit the market. Or, I may wish to hold the position and ride to more profits. My losses have been limited, so my greed is free to run. The final portion of the trade is the "Trend." By phasing into or out of positions, fear and greed are balanced, and I am able to focus on the numbers and the indicators and make money.

Emotional balance is very important to trading. Brad Johnson, a famous floor trader from the S&P pit, said it best: "Money flows in direct proportion to a trader's emotional net worth." Having the analysis right is just not enough. To win, you must keep your emotions from destroying your trade.

Avoid the "Victim" Mentality

Some traders never take personal responsibility for their trades. They always see themselves as victims of the market. Until you take personal responsibility for your trading, you will not improve. Admitting errors is not easy. A loss seems more bearable if it is someone else's fault. The trader looking for a scapegoat might say, "A friend gave me that tip. Boy, is he an idiot!" Or, "I listened to the talking heads on CNN and they missed the mark." Or, "Those hot stocks in that blog cost me thousands." It is easy to put the blame on others and hard to admit that that you took the trade and you alone bear responsibility for it—win or lose.

You are the person who decides whether to act on those tips or let them die. You are the person who clicks the mouse or phones the broker. You are the person who decides to risk your capital or not. The responsibility for the trade does not lie with your friend—it lies with you. If you hear some advice on television, check it out. Does it seem sound? Are you willing to take the trade? If so, you take and you manage it. The person acting on the advice is not sitting behind a desk on CNN; he is sitting in front of your computer, and that is the guy who bears full responsibility for the trade. Traders who pass the buck and do not accept personal responsibility for their trades do not improve. With each failure, they blame someone else and repeat their faulty actions again and again.

However, traders who own their trades are able to analyze them and improve them. That is the strategy that results in success.

Be Confident

The market will pay you what you believe that you are worth. If you think that you are a bad trader, the market will agree with your assessment. If you believe in your abilities and approach each and every trade with an attitude of confidence, the market will respect your skills and pay for them. Believe in yourself and your trade. If you do not have faith in the trade or faith in your ability to execute the trade properly, do not make the trade. It takes confidence to trade successfully. Look at the numbers, read the tape, check the time of day, and consider the risk associated with the trade. If all aspects of the trade are not in sync, wait for a better chance. Never put money on the line unless you believe that the trade will make money. Those who expect to lose will lose. They will sabotage themselves in some way. Get a winning strategy. Test it and verify that it will work. Then have confidence in it and in yourself.

Focus

Trading requires focus. I learned many years ago that if an event in my life is preventing me from being focused on my trading, I should not trade. There are times when we are angry or upset or ill that we just cannot watch the numbers and do a good job of analyzing them. An argument with the wife or kids, a night when we could not sleep, the illness or death of a close friend—all of these and dozens of other events will interfere with our ability to concentrate and focus. Therefore, if something is throwing you off and preventing you from paying attention to your trading, do not trade. Take a rest. It is best to stay out of the market for a few days than to trade and lose money. Trading is a tough game. It requires your best.

Sometimes a break from trading is good. After a big loss or a series of losses, take a rest. Do not trade for a week or so and clear your head. Rethink your strategies. Study your mistakes. Try to identify the errors that were made and vow to stop making them in the future. Write down what steps you will take when you start trading again to turn your trading around. When you go back to the market, approach it gingerly. Take small positions with little risk. Take pride in every victory. As your confidence grows, increase your positions and get bolder. Sometimes we all need to go back to the basics and get a refresher course to help us stay disciplined and profitable.

PEARL 29

Some days, your best trading decision may be to stay in bed.

There Is No Substitute for Preparation

Begin planning for the trading week on Saturday and Sunday. Use that time to study the markets and gain a mental picture of prices. In relation to the annual open, are prices up or down? For the current month, are prices up or down? During the last week, what happed with prices? Find support and resistance levels and consider trading strategies to use them effectively. Take the time to check an economic calendar and plan out your upcoming schedule. Know when major news is expected and learn what the experts are predicting. Are numbers expected to be good or bad?

When each morning begins, spend a few minutes gathering important numbers. What was the Globex open, yesterday's high and low, and other important prices? Write them down and devise a strategy around them. Can the current market be classified as a bull market or a bear one? If bullish, be careful if going short, and vice versa. You do not want to buck the trend. It is best to go with the trend and ride the market's wave.

If you are well prepared when that opening bell rings, you will be a better trader. You will be ready to take advantage of winning opportunities. The market will not take you by surprise. Preparation will also keep you from taking bad trades. You will know the traps that may be lurking in the numbers.

Knowledge Is Priceless

During a recent trip to Chicago, I spoke with Paul Eppen, an executive with OptionsXpress. Paul is a believer in education and said that success breeds ignorance. That is, traders experience some success and then they give up on learning new strategies and approaches. They think they know everything there is to know and they are content to stay in their safety zone. Maybe that fact helps explain the short life of floor traders. To survive in the markets, a person must continue to learn and adapt to new environments. Those who do not continue to learn will be short timers.

There have been so many changes in the financial markets within the last few years. Those who have not continued to learn and update their skills have been left behind. They are like fossils drying out in a field, interesting but no longer vital. The only way to keep current with technology and products is to continue to learn and upgrade skills. There are so many ways to gain knowledge. The exchanges like the Chicago Mercantile Exchange (CME) offer courses and seminars. Go to www.cme.com and check out the offerings in their education center. Brokerage houses also try to help traders and educate them. For example, visit the OptionsXpress site and click on the education tab. There are also financial forums and conferences where a great deal of information is disseminated. At DTI and other educational centers, the skills of trading are taught to students from beginners to advanced traders. There is no substitute for knowledge.

The learning process can begin at home. One of the best ways to gain knowledge is to analyze yourself and your trades. I believe that most of us learn far more from our mistakes than we do from our successes. Therefore, it is important to study each and every trade. I recommend that at the end of each day you evaluate both your good and bad trades. Get a journal and begin the process. After the markets close, find a quiet spot and write down each trade that was made. Then think about it in detail. If the trade was a winner, why did it succeed? If money was lost, why was it lost? At what time was the trade made? What did the market look like at that time? Consider the indicators, the key numbers, the manner of execution. In considering the winners, how could more money have been made? When pondering the losers, what mistakes were made and what action could have been taken to get a better result? Did you follow your rules? Exhibit discipline? Use good money management skills?

PEARL 30

Learn how to win from your losing trades.

After identifying your strengths and weaknesses, make a plan for the next day. What can be done to improve tomorrow's trading? Then put that knowledge into practice. Even though you scrutinize all aspects of your trading on a regular basis, I suggest that your rules not be changed until Saturday. The rationale behind this recommendation is that traders who continuously change the rules are undisciplined and losers. In the quiet of the weekend, consider the rules and why you use them. Do they work or not? If not, why not? Are you, in fact, employing them consistently and properly? If you determine that you need to alter some of your trading rules, set out in writing exactly what is being changed and why. Then try the new rules for a week and evaluate them. Did they improve your trading? If so—great! If not, time for more evaluation and consideration.

PEARL 31

Change your trading rules only on Saturday.

REVIEW

Trading involves far more than analyzing numbers and studying charts. There is more to do than read an indicator or check a clock. All of these are important, but trading also requires a great deal of discipline and psychological balance. Without discipline, you will trade too much and not follow any established rules or tested strategies. You will not manage your money or limit your risk. Being a good trader involves more than knowing how to trade. It requires carrying out the plan or strategy effectively and consistently.

In addition to discipline, to be a winning trader you also must have a psychological edge. You must have confidence in yourself and your abilities, but you must not have too much confidence. Most of us are bit players on a big stage. Our financial resources are too limited to control the market. All we can do is identify how the market is moving and join the move. Arrogance when dealing with the markets will not put money in the bank.

The biggest emotional dilemma that traders face is balancing greed and fear. We all want to make money, but being greedy generally results in poor judgment and losing trades. Fear keeps us out of trades or pushes us into accepting unnecessary losses. The bottom line is simple: make money, but do not be greedy. Respect the market, but do not be fearful of it.

CHAPTER 19

The Last Word

When I look back over my trading career, I feel somewhat like a fossil. I am in my mid-fifties, but when it comes to trading, I have been around a long time. Most traders, especially those who do a lot of day trading, do not survive for the long haul. It is well known that the professional life span of floor traders is short and often not so sweet. I have never been a floor trader, but I have been a broker, a trading educator, and a professional trader managing my own finances. I am like the bunny on television that advertises batteries—I just keep on ticking.

My trading history has not always been easy. I have seen my fair share of hard times and losses. Wall Street has landed a few solid blows. My darkest days were the ones following Black Monday in 1987. My mistakes were very costly, and coming to terms with my personal errors as well as inherent issues with the markets themselves took time. In fact, it took me a few years to regain my footing and move on to better things. I succeeded because I did not give up and I educated myself anew and learned more about trading and about the markets.

If you are looking for a trading system that involves five easy steps, you will not find it in the pages of this book. In fact, you will not find it anywhere. Systems do not work because financial markets are always in a state of flux. A programmed trade that worked on Monday may not work on Tuesday because the markets are not the same. The markets are constantly adjusting, adapting, and changing. It is not only prices that move, but the general economy and the mind-set of traders. The only way to be effective over the long term is to learn and adapt as things change. There are periods of time when the average true range (ATR) on the E-mini S&P futures is only 9 or 10 points in the course of a session. At the time of this writing, that same range is about 20 points. The changing environment mandates a slightly different strategy. That is only one example of how the markets change.

From many years of experience, I have developed a trading strategy that centers on time, key numbers, and market indicators. I use time in a number of helpful ways. First and foremost, I take a global approach. Trading goes on somewhere in the world virtually 24 hours a day. The most active trading centers follow the path of the sun as it makes its way across the sky from east to west. Asian traders have the first shot at the day. When we are enjoying Sunday evening, traders in China, Japan, Singapore, and other Asia trading centers are busy buying and selling. When Asian exchanges wind down, Europe gets going. By the time most U.S. traders get ready to make their first trade of the day, many parts of the world have looked at the markets, evaluated them, traded them, and shut them down. I use that knowledge to add more depth and insight into my trading. If a buying wave is spreading from Asia and Europe to the United States, I will be ready to surf it. Likewise, I will be prepared if I see a sell-off coming my way.

I also use time to help me select the best moments to place my trades. I know that some times during the day have the right volume and volatility to allow my trades to pay. Therefore, I trade during these times and stay out of the market when the odds of success are not in my favor. In addition to getting into the markets at the right time, I also want to be out of the action when the time is wrong. If markets are flat or unpredictable, I sit on the side lines and wait for better opportunities.

Another vital aspect of my trading method is key numbers. To make money trading, you have to know and use key numbers. These numbers point the way for buying and selling at the ideal time. They also identify price points for placement of stop/loss orders. Markets tend to move up and down between key numbers. Therefore, knowing them helps you stay clear of bad trades and gain more consistency. It is painful to buy the top or sell the bottom. However, traders who do not use key numbers often do just that.

To help me stay on the right side of the action, I rely on the Seven Sisters, a group of indexes that keep me on track. Specifically, I track the equity index futures, including the S&P 500 futures, the Dow 30 futures, and the Nasdaq 100 futures. I also follow the German Dax futures. To add more breadth to my analysis, I watch gold, bonds, and oil futures. By using the Seven Sisters, I have a good view of the action of the overall market.

Finally, I rely on market indicators. Before I put my hard-earned cash at risk, I want to be certain that the odds of success are in my favor. I want to see the New York Stock Exchange (NYSE) tick moving my way. I want confirmation from the Nasdaq and NYSE issues, and I want the other indicators like the TTick and V-Factor giving me a warm and fuzzy feeling.

I use time, key numbers, and market indicators to execute all of my strategies. Whether I am trading stocks, futures, options, bonds, or commodities, I select the right time, rely on key numbers to lead the way, and seek confirmation from market indicators.

The most difficult part of trading is that it is not a one, two, three-step process. Trading is an art, and like a painting or a sculpture, there are many variations and nuances. That is why learning and education are so important. To a large degree, you have to sense what is happening and react to it.

In addition to mastering a particular strategy or game plan, there are many other skills that come to play in the art of trading. If you want to be a winner, you need to be disciplined and follow your strategy day in and day out. You need persistence so that you are not emotionally defeated by each loss. You must have the ability to trade without becoming greedy or overtaken by fear. If you get too arrogant, your arrogance will cause you to lose your perspective and, with it, your analysis and ability to make good trading decisions. When you are wrong, you will not be able to admit it and the result will be financial ruin.

Another critical aspect of any trading strategy is risk management. You cannot trade with abandon and lose track of your money. If you do so, you will not be trading for the long haul. Manage every trade and keep losses low. If you experience a number of bad trades in succession, quit trading. Get away from the market and spend time analyzing the problem.

If there is one message that you must take away from this book, it is the importance of education. The markets change, and as they do, so must you. Education is the key to being able to adapt to any market and make money. If you want further guidance, you may wish to obtain a DVD that DTI has prepared, *The Trader's Edge*. This DVD gives some additional specific approaches to trading today's markets. Visit the web site at www.dtitrader.com for more information and a reader's discount.

I hope the strategies and insights that you have learned from these pages will be helpful. Keep studying the markets and learning about them. Knowledge pays!

Resources

WEB SITES

www.dtitrader.com
www.optionsXpress.com
www.barrons.com
www.forexfactory.com
www.dtn.com
www.PensonGHCO.com
www.naphill.org
www.osoktrading.com
www.CMEGroup.com
www.MoneyShow.com
www.MarketEDU.com
www.bizradio.com

SUGGESTED READING

Busby, Tom. *Winning the Day Trading Game*. Hoboken, NJ: John Wiley & Sons, 2005.

Busby, Tom. *The Markets Never Sleep*. Hoboken, NJ: John Wiley & Sons, 2007.

Hill, Napoleon. *Think and Grow Rich*. San Diego, CA: Aventine Press, 2004 (originally published in 1937).

Hirsch, Jeffrey, and Yale Hirsch. *Stock Trader's Almanac*. Hoboken, NJ: John Wiley & Sons, 2004.

Roosevelt, Ruth Barrons. *12 Habitudes of Highly Successful Traders*. Greenville, SC: Traders Press, 2001.

Smitten, Richard. *Jesse Livermore: World's Greatest Stock Trader*. Hoboken, NJ: John Wiley & Sons, 2001.

About the Authors

Thomas L. Busby, the founder and CEO of DTI, has been a professional securities trader for more than 25 years. He began his trading career with Merrill Lynch, and before DTI opened its doors in 1996, he was a vice president with Salomon Smith Barney.

Tom earned a bachelor's degree in business administration from the University of Georgia and a juris doctorate degree from Oklahoma City University School of Law. He was a distinguished graduate of the United States Air Force Budget Officer School, and served seven years as an officer in the United States Air Force prior to becoming a professional securities broker and trader. Tom is well respected in his field and is a member of both the Chicago Mercantile Exchange (CME) and the Chicago Board of Trade (CBOT).

Tom suffered a great financial setback during the crash of 1987. When the market tanked, he was overleveraged in the options market. Many traders would have left the arena after such a loss, but not Tom. He persisted and immersed himself in his work by studying and analyzing the markets. Out of his defeat came a new determination to improve his approach and become a better trader. Over the years he has developed a unique method whereby the avoidance of risk has become his primary focus and profit taking has assumed a second-row seat. This approach has served him and his students well. Tom's trading method incorporates more than two decades of experience; he is a veteran of many bullish as well as bearish cycles, and he freely shares his knowledge and experience with his students.

Tom is a frequent contributor to a variety of trading publications. Over the years Tom has written many articles covering a wide array of trading topics. He is also the co-author of *Winning the Day Trading Game* and *The Markets Never Sleep*, both published by John Wiley and Sons.

Tom and his wife, Paula, have been married for more than two decades. Their sons, Winston and Morgan, are also traders and work with their father at DTI.

Patsy Busby Dow holds a juris doctorate degree from Tulane School of Law. She is a former assistant district attorney and a former assistant United States attorney. Several years ago, when making a career change, she began learning the art of trading. Tom Busby was, of course, her mentor. Patsy is coauthor of *Winning the Day Trading Game* and *The Markets Never Sleep*. In addition to her degree in law and her trading education, Patsy also holds a master's degree in education and a master's degree in history from the University of South Alabama. She has been married for 38 years to Mike Dow, a former four-term mayor for the city of Mobile, and they have three children.

Index